STOP

feeding crazy
& pursue peace

How to Heal from Broken Relationships

STOP

feeding crazy & pursue peace

How to Heal From Broken Relationships

DARVIN LEWIS

Darvin Lewis
Publishing

Printed in the United States of America.

First Edition Printed May 2013.

Some names have been changed to protect the identities of those involved in the events described.

Library of Congress Control Number: 2013905290

ISBN 10: 0-9891709-0-X

ISBN 13: 978-0-9891709-0-1

For granny, who showed me nothing was impossible.

CONTENTS

ACKNOWLEDGEMENTS

Thank you to all those who encouraged me along the way. Your loving words were appreciated. God Bless you all.

"A time will come, however, indeed it is already here, when the true (genuine) worshipers will worship the Father in spirit and in truth (reality); for the Father is seeking just such people as these as his worshipers." - John 4:24

INTRODUCTION

---

the truth

The truth is that I come to you a true sinner. I've done everything in life I thought I was big and bad enough to do. I have slept around, smoked this and that, did lines of cocaine, popped pills, been so drunk I thought I was going to die. I have cussed at my parents, fussed with my family, said a lot of things I am not necessarily proud of, done a lot of things I wish I had not done; but the truth is that I am not afraid to tell it.

Lately I've been so sick and tired of people trying to give out advice but no one wants to admit to their own misdeeds. No one wants to admit what they went through or where they came from. Some Christians today can't decide if they want to tell you where they've really come from but they want to preach about where you should be going.

The truth is most people know they need to "get right," but I believe that a lot of people could better relate if somebody just stood up and told the honest to God's truth about who they are and what they've gone through, and the struggle they continue to go through. So here I am, uninhibited and raw, naked before you with my piece of truth.

Now maybe you won't like the book, maybe you will. Maybe you'll send me an email telling me that I'm going to Hell or a message asking me who I think I am. Who knows? At the end of the day none of that even matters because the truth...the truth is that I know this book is going to help somebody. I know that somewhere in this world there is a boy, a man just like me who needs somebody to say what I am about to say: I am a gay man. I have lived my life for the past fourteen years as a gay man. I am also attracted to women. I feel as though one day I might even actually marry a woman and have a family, but that hasn't happened yet, and may never happen. That area is one that God is still working with me on. I'm not perfect. Nobody is. But I want *you* to know that I know that I'm not perfect before you go any further with this book; because this book *is* my truth.

I've been beat up, had my teeth knocked out, strung out, arms broken, unemployed, heartbroken, and out of luck. You name it. I've been there in some form or fashion. And now here I am, far from perfect, but still here. I'm a little bit wiser, a little bit tougher, a lot more spiritual, and more in tune with what God wants from me. I know that He wants this book to come forth. I know that there is a word in here for somebody. I know that somewhere somebody has been waiting on somebody to just be real, so here I am.

Like I said, I come to you a sinner, but a sinner that is trying to find his way in life. I make no promises that I am some biblical expert. I am not one of those heavenly bound Christian leaders who can rattle off scripture on a whim and cast down demons in front of your face, or pretend to by pushing somebody to the ground (whichever you choose to believe). I'm just me. I've come through some things, made it through some storms and I've learned a few lessons along the way. I'm a lot smarter than I was ten years ago, and I have experienced enough of God's grace to feel compelled to share my journey with you thus far.

I know enough to say God loves you, that He is real, that His love is real, and that He wants what's best for you. It's that simple.

This book is about healing from broken relationships, but ultimately this will never happen if you don't build a relationship with God first. So how do you do that? Well, the first step is salvation. If you're not saved get saved right now. Roman's 10:9 says that if you confess with your mouth Jesus is Lord, and believe in your heart that God raised him from the dead, you will be saved. It's that simple.

God's word is true, and there is no need for you to walk around feeling as though you're not wanted or loved, or that you're all alone in life. God wants to walk with you and He is willing to do so if you would just confess those words and believe them in your heart.

Now if I don't get anything else across to you in this book you just know that God loves you. He's there for you, He hears you, He sees you, and He has not forgotten you. Relationships are hard but you are not alone. God loves you. He loves you, He loves you, He loves you. He has not forsaken you. We all have things to learn but it will be okay. So if you're still game get ready to turn the page and we will take this ride together.

Now who knows what we'll find at the end but I hope it's a little peace, a little wisdom, and a little joy as we heal from our brokenness and re-connect our relationships with God, our Lord and Saviour Jesus Christ. And to that I say Amen.

REFLECTION QUESTIONS

What are the skeletons in your closet you feel others might judge you by if they knew the truth about you?

In other words, if there was one thing about you that you could keep others from knowing, what would that one thing be?

And now...how to heal from broken relationships

CHAPTER ONE

—

pre-existing conditions

I had lain in bed for days. I had barely moved. The windows were closed, sheets hung over the blinds to block out even more sunlight. My seventy-five-year-old grandmother was downstairs, most-likely sitting in her pink chair in the corner of the dining room, dressed in a robe spotted with brown-crusted cigarette burns. I imagine she had her hands crossed, placed in her lap as she stared at the "old school" floor model television set, unaware that her beloved grandson was laying in bed upstairs drenched in a blanket of despair and depression.

Life had unraveled for me. I found myself at an impasse, a crossroads, unaware of what direction I should go in. I had no plan, no future, and no outline for my life. All I knew at this moment was that I was lost. I was unemployed, gay, and an un-admitted alcoholic slash heavy drug-user. I had just recently broken up with my boyfriend who happened to be HIV positive after he had nearly killed me one night by accident in a drunken fit. I was heartbroken. I was ravaged, beaten up, bruised, beat down, betrayed by love, outfoxed by the streets, and outdone by this thing called life. In other words...I was a mess.

How had I allowed this to happen to me? I was suppose to be the golden child of the family. I was the prodigal son who had in all fairness been given everything.

My grandmother, Mary Lewis, had raised me as her own since I had been a baby, lavishing me with whatever my heart desired. She did her best to place me in good Catholic schools and attempted to shelter me from the evils of the world, or at least that's how she liked to tell it.

There is, however, always another side to the truth. The truth is that my grandmother had spent the majority of her life struggling to make ends meet. She had raised four children predominantly as a single mother, and she had made plenty of mistakes along the way. She was not a woman you would have called soft and cuddly. She didn't give people big bear hugs nor did she throw around words like "I love you."

Nevertheless, she did know how to work. She knew how to survive. She knew how to pay bills and prepare meals that would feed a family for days. She knew how to construct a home and provide stability. My grandmother had common sense, and she had a brain that worked. She valued education and she understood the dilemmas that little black children faced in the world. She was practical, pragmatic, and even more important; she was the primary mother figure in my life. This woman was my number one fan...You know that one person in life (if you've been so blessed) who believes in you blindly. Nothing you do or ask is too much, and they almost seem joyful to bear the burden of loving you.

Now, I don't have children, but if I did I imagine I would feel this way: I imagine I would strive to make their lives better and would want to give them the best of me. I would want their lives to be enlightened and made better because they knew me. It was paternal love, unwavering, and biased in my favor.

My grandmother adored me in her own special way. I felt it. I knew what she was trying to do. She was trying to love me. Of course there were those in my family who criticized her for loving me too much. They called her love for me "perverted" and "not right."

I can remember being a child, no more than six or seven years old and having no idea what they meant by this, although I sensed a strange and negative storm brewing around me.

By now my two aunts had their own families, my uncle was living his own sad life, and my father had gotten married and had relocated to Michigan with his new wife and her daughter. Meanwhile my own mother, my maternal mother was living in the same city as me but was in my life only on a part-time basis.

You see I was never sure why I ended up where I did. No one had ever told me the story about why I had been left with my grandmother for all those years. No one bothered to explain it, but maybe had they known about my developing condition of "why" and "how come" they would have been more forthcoming.

How did I end up at my grandmother's house but my sister, only a year and a half younger than I had been allowed to stay with my mother? What did I do? What was wrong with me? Why wasn't I allowed to be with my mother?

These questions burned in my soul and festered in my spirit for decades. Why, what, and how come? What did I do and what was wrong with me? What was it? Did I do something? Could you not afford me? Was the love between my mother and father not strong enough to withstand the weight of me as a child? Were they too young when they had me? Were they too smart or too dumb? How come and why had no one explained this to me? Didn't I deserve to know the truth about me, my history, my story, my condition? Didn't I deserve to know all of it...Didn't I?

My father tried to explain it to me once when I was older and what it came down to was this: He said that my grandmother took one look at me and fell in love. That was all it took and she knew that she had to have me. He told me that he and my mother weren't able to take care of a newborn and so they did the best they could do. My father enlisted in the Air Force and the plan was for my grandmother to help out with the new baby until the two of them could get on their feet.

He said everything was going fine for a while and then came the trickery. My father said that one day while he was still stationed at Fort Bragg in North Carolina he received an envelope stuffed with a stack of papers. He told me that when he realized these papers were documents naming my grandmother as my new legal guardian he immediately called my grandmother to ask her why she had sent these to him. Apparently my grandmother told him that I had been sick on and off again, and that she had been unable to make any real medical decisions because she was not listed as my primary guardian.

Now of course this makes sense. My father was stationed in North Carolina and I was living with my grandmother in Indianapolis. If anything was to happen to me while I was in her care she would be unable to make any emergency decisions. However, my father said something didn't quite gel with what she was saying. He said something felt odd and so he told my grandmother to wait just a little while longer until he returned home and then they would talk it through.

Now this is where it gets sticky. My father told me that it was not very long after this that he received another set of documents, this time signed and certified. These were the same legal documents my grandmother had sent the first time only this time they contained the signatures of my mother and my father, only neither of my parents had ever signed these papers. He said my grandmother had forged their signatures and had found a way to get what she wanted—me.

Now I don't know if my father's explanation was the truth or just his version of what happened. The truth is that I have never sat down with my mother and discussed the situation with her, and my grandmother has since gone on to glory as she would call it. So the truth is that we will never know the truth, but I do know this: I know that my grandmother loved me and those around her the best way she knew how.

Now I'm sure that a large part of the reason that she did what she did was due to the fact that she wanted a redo in life, as most people do. I'm sure that when she saw me she saw an opportunity to somehow correct the mistakes she had made in her past. By the time I came along she was financially stable, owned her own home, and was in a position to do for me in a way she had never been able to for her own children. I imagine she wanted to see what it felt like the second time around.

She did it out of love and for a chance to somehow mend her own broken past. She gave me the best of who she was, unaware that her love was helping to feed a developing condition within myself. For in the midst of her love was the brooding power of the ego. This was made evident by the selfishness she exhibited by her attempts to detour me from a meaningful relationship with my mother which is what I longed for.

I can remember going to church with my grandmother when I was little. I can recall seeing a woman in the choir stands that resembled my mother. I remember being fixated on this woman throughout the entire worship service. When the minister finished preaching and had delivered the final benediction I remember edging my way down the aisle towards this woman as she left the choir stands, finally calling out to her "Momma!"

My grandmother laughed the whole thing off, but if anyone had paid closer attention to me they would have seen a little boy desperate to be with his mother. I was desperate to be held, loved on, tucked away, and made to feel safe in my mother's arms.

Perhaps my grandmother did notice and chose not to say anything. I don't know, but what I do know is that in that moment I felt like a motherless child.

I didn't know that my situation was nothing special, nor the circumstances unique. I had no idea that there were millions of other little black boys, and white boys, and Hispanic boys all over the world who felt the same way I did. I didn't know there was an epidemic of absentee mothers and fathers in the world who had either willingly or unwillingly bestowed their child-rearing responsibilities on the grandparents of the world. I thought I was the only one.

You see in her quest to love me she isolated me, tucked me away like a prisoner and threw away the key. I was never allowed to go very far. I was due in the house the moment the street lights came on even if it wasn't dark. I remember not being able to leave the yard even though we only owned a small parcel of land. If it was summertime she would say it was too hot to go outside, and if the snow fell she would say it was too cold. It was always something.

Apparently I was not the only one who thought this was strange. My Father and my aunts had all expressed their resentment to my grandmother at one time or another. They would advise her with phrases like "Let him be a child!" and "What are you keeping him in the house for?"

If my grandmother regretted not being there enough for her own children she made up for it with me. She was there at every turn, incessantly. At times it felt as though it was just she and I against the world. It was as though we were alone in the universe and all we had to lean on was each other.

Sometimes she made it seem as though she was doing us all a favor by being the responsible one, by caring for me because nobody else wanted to.

However, the truth was that I was often times made to feel as though my mother was the boogeyman coming to get me. I didn't understand what made my mother so bad, but to say my grandmother was discontent with my mother would be an understatement. I was confused by the whole thing. Was I not supposed to love my mother? Was I not good enough to be loved in return?

I felt as though my own mother was holding some sort of grudge against me, only no one had ever told me what I had done wrong. I felt abandoned. Yes there were moments, days, even weeks here and there when I did have a chance to spend time with my mother and her side of the family. It was a vacation to me. These people, my other people were totally different. They laughed together, talked to each other, spent time together, dare I say even liked each other too. They would fellowship together, eat together, lived on top of one another but rarely complained about it. They were tight. If one had a spot then they all had a spot. It was different. They loved on you, smiled at you and made you feel like you had someplace to call your own. It was comfortable. It felt the way you'd want home to feel—warm, gentle, full of life, and accepting of who you are. Only my real home, my other home was on the other side of town. And when the weekend and summer visits had ended I found myself being dropped off in front of my grandmother's house, torn.

I was glad to be back because this was the place that I knew as home. I was spoiled here. Everything was mine and who wouldn't want that? Yet before the night was over and probably just after I had taken my bath I declare a few tears would gather in the corner of my eyes, longing for my other people and that feeling of being where you belong.

I had unknowingly developed a condition of unbalance. At the time I had no idea that this search for balance would become one of my greatest ambitions in life. I had already begun contemplating who and what might be able to fill this void that was growing inside me.

Yes, my grandmother had loved me, but it was not a balanced love. Her love had been skewed to serve only a portion of who I was. The other part of me had been left unattended, deprived of a love that no man or thing could fill, no matter how well-intentioned they might have been.

I should have been loved equally by my mother, my father, my grandmother, but I didn't get that. I felt a lot of love from my grandmother and a little love from my mother, but a little love wasn't enough. I wanted the whole thing. I wanted to *feel* the love of my mother. I wanted to know that I was loved by her completely. Instead I had question marks, shadows, areas of my brain dredged with confusion. I felt alone, isolated, mixed up, turned around, and the older I got the more I sought someone who could unravel me.

I went looking for love, searching for an answer, someone that would complete me, make me whole.

And then love found me. There I was seventeen years old, fresh out of high school. I was hanging out at a coffee house late one night with my best friend. It was nearly summertime. The air was slightly cool but still comfortable. I saw a young man standing by a brown Jeep Cherokee. He was slim, not too tall, wore contacts that looked like cat eyes. I thought he was cute and he must have thought I was okay too. It didn't take long before he offered me and my best friend a ride home.

My best friend and I hopped in the backseat of the SUV. The young man introduced us to his other two friends who were inside as well.

"Isn't he cute?" he commented, looking at me.

Then the young man in the front passenger seat looked back at us over his shoulder, his sunglasses resting on the spot just before the tip of his nose.

"Hmm," the young man grinned, "Yes he is."

And that was it. I didn't know it then but love had found me, and his name was JC. We would start off as acquaintances then work our way to friends, gradually laying down complex layers of life and laughter, secrets and mischief. It was the beginning of a six year hurricane that would leave me spent. It was the beginning of our love story, for this young man would prove to be the one—the one I would risk my life for, nearly lose my mind over and be forced to recover from. It was the beginning of a future that would be steeped in alcoholism, drug use, late nights and early mornings.

I came to him broken but I left brokenhearted. I had found someone just as sick as I was to love and so we tried to love on each other in our own sick way. I was battered on the inside, reeling from the effects of my decision to love him. I loved this boy to a fault, overlooking the devastation that the time we spent together was having on my life. I was blinded by my condition and so I loved him and lost myself in the process.

This boy was my world and for years I crawled through the mud and the thick thinking that something worthwhile was going to come of it all. Have you ever done that? Have you ever crawled through the thick of life for someone thinking you were going to change them and come out clean on the other side? Have you ever placed your hope in someone...else? I wanted to be with him but it was not meant to be. But more about this story later. For now we'll go back to my condition.

My condition of unbalance had allowed me to lose myself and misplace my spirit in the midst of my mess. I had overlooked the importance of slowing down, communicating my problems and my fears with those that really mattered.

15

You see I should have confronted my father, my mother, my grandmother. I should have laid it all on the table and told them how I was feeling, but I didn't do that. I should have confronted the problem head-on so we could all move on, but that's not what I did either. That's not what most of us do, no. We like to carry things around, dress them up, call it name brand baggage and hope that because our baggage looks pretty no one will notice that it's still just that—baggage.

I, like so many others ran around and away thinking I'd find myself somewhere along the way.

You see sometimes in life you develop these things called conditions, and these conditions can go by many names. Sometimes it is a condition of an absentee father, or a home filled with drugs and alcohol. Sometimes the condition is called abuse, neglect, abandonment, sexual misconduct. Whatever the condition the effect is the same.

The first symptom is usually a broken spirit. Our lives become puzzles scattered about and we search for someone to help us put ourselves back together again. Only the one thing many of us come to realize is that we didn't lose or misplace ourselves or these missing pieces, no. Sometimes we just gave them away.

This realization can occur gradually or in an instant. You may realize suddenly or over a period of time that you have been either consciously or subconsciously retracing your steps, going from place to place, from person to person, from bad choice to other bad choices trying to find yourself again.

Hopefully this book will be something like a map for you as you set out on this conscious journey of self-discovery. But before you embark on this journey you must first ask yourself some preliminary questions and diagnose any and all pre-existing conditions you may have.

For instance, have you been running from something in your past? If so who, and why? Are there any unanswered questions you have for loved ones or those from your past?

What were those questions? Did you mean to have some awkward conversation with your parents and never got around to it? What is at the bottom of your condition? What were the stimulants, the factors that contributed the condition you are in now? Think about it. What is *your* pre-existing condition? We've all come from somewhere but it's up to us to be honest with ourselves about where that place was, how dirty it was, and why we wanted to escape that place so badly. You must determine your history. There is no way around it.

Insurance companies deny claims for coverage if you have a pre-existing medical condition, so why in the world would anyone in their right mind want to deal with us and our pre-existing emotional, spiritual, and mental conditions when we haven't taken the time to work them out.

If you go to the doctor they ask you a series of questions about your medical history, not just to be nosey, but so they know the best way to treat you. The same principle applies to life. Your past is the key to your future, and the moment you decide to get real with yourself is the moment you'll be one step closer to freedom, and that my friend is what this is all about.

REFLECTION QUESTIONS

What are the white elephants of your life?

What issues do you carry from childhood, or from other past relationships that you know have negatively affected you, or have gone without some kind of closure?

What are the unanswered questions of your life?

CHAPTER TWO

---

scar tissue

When we are children we hear our parents call out to us, "Don't run, you'll fall! Be careful!" And then in perfect timing we take that plunge and we fall. Sometimes we skin our knees, our chins, our elbows. We scream and carry on, and we watch as our wound is tended to. We get a band-aid placed over the cut and we sit down just long enough to build up the courage to start running again, only to heed the same warning, "Don't run, you'll fall! Be careful! Watch where you're going!"

It's a vicious cycle for a four-year-old but eventually we get the hang of it. If we run and we're not careful to watch where we're going or what we're doing we will eventually hurt ourselves in the process. The same principle applies to life.

A lot of us arc running around and we're not really watching where we're going or what we're doing. We spend an incredible amount of time getting back on our feet instead of staying in one spot long enough to let our wounds heal.

Some of us don't believe fat means greasy as my grandmother use to say. We like to run our fingers through the fire just to see if it's hot. We are given ample advice, endless suggestions, and we still do not heed the warnings.

Many of us just want to do what *we* want to do, optimistic that our circumstances will somehow trump time-tested wisdom.

Like most people in the world I tend to know the right thing to do, but it doesn't mean I necessarily do it. I smoked cigarettes for years, Newport 100's in a box so they wouldn't get bent in my pocket. At one point I was smoking three packs a day. I knew that smoking was bad for me. I had tried to quit since I was a junior in high school, one time dramatically dumping an entire box of cigarettes in the toilet, only to rush to the store a few hours later to buy more.

It took me twelve years before I finally quit smoking cigarettes even though I knew better all along. But I wanted to be a part of the in-crowd. I wanted to be a part of the popular clique in high school. I wanted to give them something to talk about, something that would make them say "Hey, look at him. Isn't he cool? Look at what he's doing. Isn't he something?"

I wanted to fit in and so I did something that put my health at risk and ended up costing me thousands of dollars over the years. And for what—some good times and a few laughs? I could have saved myself a lot of time and trouble had I not been so eager to fit in or so quick to give in to my fleshly desires. Yet it seems that this is the unrelenting plight of our humanness, our endless struggle—to conquer, filter, sort, and ultimately subdue those desires we know we should not embrace but continue to long for.

Jesus said it best when He commented to His disciples in Gethsemane saying, **"The spirit is indeed willing, but the flesh is weak."**

It is during these moments of temptation that we are reminded of our resounding carnal instincts and the endless work we must do in order to curb these fleshly desires. Yet despite the weight of this sin-induced burden the way is made exceedingly clear. There is no guesswork involved.

The Bible says **"I call heaven and earth to witness this day against you that I have set before you life and death, the blessings and the curses; therefore choose life, that you and your descendants may live,"** reads Deuteronomy 30:19.

The operative word in this passage is the word "choose." We have to choose to do the right thing in the midst of a situation where we could do wrong. The fact is the flesh always wants more, but we have to learn to give it what it needs and not what it always wants.

Most of the things people regret in their lives are not things they were forced to do, but things they *chose* to do, places they *chose* to go, people they *chose* to see or stay friends with. We gamble our destinies, our futures, our livelihoods in the name of love, lust, drunken nights, or moments when possibility meets fearlessness. These are the moments we conjure up the nerve to step outside our boxes and into the world to do things we would have never done, sometimes paying the price the rest of our lives.

Some of us hate to be at home alone because doing so makes us feel lonely. Instead of planning things to do with our time we wait until the loneliness is palpable, or we wait until we're so bored that we can't stand the idea of being at home for one more minute. This leads to a host of other bad choices and bad decisions that could have been avoided had we given it a little foresight and a little extra effort.

Now this situation would not be so bad the first, second, or even the third time it took place. God knows change takes time. The problem, however, develops when situations like this become ongoing patterns.

The Bible says "So any person who knows what is right to do but does not do it, to him it is sin," reads James **4:17.**

This scripture is so wonderful because it adapts to our varying situations. The key phrase in this scripture are the words "who knows better." This lets us know that we won't always know what the right choice to make. Nevertheless, when we do know the right path to take it is our duty to do our best to maintain the right course of action.

Choices become habitual. Doing wrong is easy and that's why so many of us take the easy way out. It's easy to have sex with somebody but it takes time and effort to get to know somebody, grow with somebody and abstain from physical intimacy. It's easy to take the shortcuts in life. It's easy to eat unhealthy foods but it takes effort to go to the grocery store and buy nutritious foods that will benefit you in the long run. All of these things take planning and patience, two qualities most of us would rather look over and ignore and pretend did not exist.

Sin feels good but the process of dying to one's self can be slow and grueling. Nevertheless, the discomfort is worth it.

Just like our parents warned us to slow down they also warned us that nothing worth having comes easy, and this is the attitude we must keep if we plan on achieving victory in our lives. You see when you fall down and you wound your knee a scab forms over the wound. This natural healing process emerges from *and* because of the very thing it is meant to protect, the same way our faith grows from *and* because of the very trials we think will overtake us.

Your mess will become your blessing. In other words...if you accept your lesson you will accept your blessing.

We have to learn to stop messing with our issues. We have to learn to stop trying to fix every problem that comes up as though we were God and know what the end will be. We have to give our wounds time to heal. We have to stop picking at our scabs.

Some of us aren't giving God time to work. We have become trapped in these vicious cycles. We are deceiving ourselves to think that by doing the same things over and over again we're going to get different results. We have become prisoners to our emotions, and so the challenge is to accept the lesson God is trying to teach us, and to get off these emotional roller coasters once and for all.

These emotional life cycles serve one of two purposes. You will either grow and become better, or you will fester, dry up and become even more bitter.

A lot of us don't realize it but there is a pattern to our emotional discomfort.

There are nine unique segments to our emotional life cycle. It may benefit you to pinpoint where you are in this process if you are planning on getting off this emotional roller coaster.

First there is the activating event, then the first-response reaction, followed by the consequential result, the consequential choice, living based on feeling, the secondary activating event, the emotional recall, the emotional reaction, and finally the emotion-based decision.

The *activating event* will be something significant and out of the norm that takes place in our lives. It could be a birth, a death; maybe someone goes to jail or prison, or anything else that can stop you cold in your tracks. This event is followed by a *first-response reaction* to whatever has happened. During these times we may give no thought at all to the consequences of our actions.

This event could induce the fight or flight response within us, when we subconsciously do whatever is necessary to survive in times of great stress or unrest.

This is followed by the *consequential result* of our actions. If you have overly-indulged in food then your consequential result could be that you pack on a few extra pounds. If you abused your children then your consequential result could be them being taken away and placed with another family member or even being placed in the foster care system.

Following this consequential result is the *consequential choice*. This is when the real growth takes place because this is the moment we decide to either grow from the experience or to blame our problems on somebody or something else. This is the moment when we decide to become bitter or better. This is the moment when we decide to either accept or reject the lesson. This is the moment our growth hinges on.

Following this consequential choice is the stage when many of us begin *living based on our feelings*. If we have accepted the opportunity to grow life will begin to change for us. We will begin to see things differently. However, if by chance you choose the alternative and you choose not to accept the lesson that life is trying to teach you, you will mostly likely find yourself repeating these same situations over again.

Once you begin living life based on these new feelings you will find yourself either bitter or better, and you will begin living life based on how you feel. These feelings will eventually trigger a *secondary activating event*.

If you've become better you should see a better result. Maybe you'll land a new job, perhaps you'll start repairing your financial affairs, or maybe it will be something as simple as cleaning your house on a more regular basis.

The same principle applies to those of us who become bitter during this period and reject the lesson that life was trying to teach us. Our lives will reflect our attitudes. Bitterness will surely bear bitter fruit, lifelessness and stagnation.

As we begin to observe our lives and we see what has occurred as a result of our belief system we will experience an *emotional recall*. We will recall where we've come from, our history, our right choices and our bad choices. We will either shout in victory or we will seep further into an emotional rut, not realizing that the energy we have taken in is now being reflected out and is giving us just what we've asked for. Our lives will become a reflection of our beliefs.

This reflection will eventually cause us to make a decision based on how worthy we feel after everything else that has happened to us in life. And so there it is: an emotional life cycle...a cycle of unworthiness.

We experience emotional recall, we act out based on these emotions, we make an emotional decision which will in turn create our activating event.

Activating Event leads to a first-response reaction then consequential result , and a consequential choice based on the result.

We begin living on our feelings which in turn creates another activating event.

The Bible says "The beginning of Wisdom is: get Wisdom (skillful and godly Wisdom)! [For skillful *and* godly Wisdom is the principal thing.] And with all you have gotten, get understanding (discernment, comprehension, and interpretation)," reads Proverbs 4:7.

God is saying get a clue! Stop running around making foolish choices and doing things you know you have no business doing. Figure out where you are in life, in this cycle. Stop blaming the people from your past for the choices you make today. Give yourself time to breathe after life has thrown you a curve ball. Slow down and take a moment to heal. Stop picking at those scabs before you end up with a scar for life.

REFLECTION QUESTIONS

Who or what were the things you rebounded from too quickly?

What were the issues in your life you feared you might never recover from if you didn't do so quickly?

What seemingly courageous actions did you take that has now come back to haunt you?

What were the things you didn't properly heal from?

CHAPTER THREE

---

be thankful

When I look back on my life I see so many places I could have ended up. I think about the nights I made it home without a clue of how I had gotten there. It seems that all our lives are summed up by one question– what if?

What if we had gone down the other road? What if we had taken *that* street home? What if we had just gone home a just few seconds earlier? What if we had not opened the door and let *that* man in? What if?

What if we had waited on our blessing a little while longer and not rushed into something? What if we had waited on God instead?

If you're reading this book then that means you must have made it through something, from someone...to this place, somewhere. And that is why God is worthy to be praised. Never mind all the other stuff. Never mind all that other mess. Never mind all those troubles and the bills, and all the other coulda, woulda, shoulda's of life that attempt to take you down if you let them. No, this is the time to stop and say "thank you." Thank you to God, to the past from which you came, for the wisdom it has given you, for the grace that has been shown and that which is sure to come. Yes, grace...that unmerited, unqualified, undeserving spiritual blessing and favor that will cause you to look back on where you've been and simply weep.

Weep...for the love lost and the love gained, for the good times and the bad, for all those things you thought you would never live without and somehow did. You made it through.

I can remember my dark days, when I was in the thick of things. My drug use had spiraled out of control. I was losing myself. The party was over. It was dangerous now. It had started out as something fun to do. It was entertaining then but now the mood was desperate. Now it had turned ugly, right side up, tilted and confused. People didn't care now. They were stingy now. What was theirs was *theirs*. People didn't share now. There was distance now, and the friends I thought were friends were not my friends at all. There was no one to call now, no visit to make, no trip to take, no shoulder to cry on. No, there was just time for healing now...Time to heal and recover from this mess that I had made.

But before I do *this,* before I go to the dark side of the moon I want to talk to you about the "good ol days." These days when my friends and I would all buy our own individual packs of cocaine and party until the sun came up the next morning.

We were all in our early-twenties then and nothing about what we were doing felt remotely wrong. It was a good time. We told ourselves that we were sewing our wild oats, and so we tried to convince ourselves that this was just something that young people did. It was an excuse for us to live life on the edge. We set out to live and get our life! We went to house parties, stayed there until the sun came up the next morning, all the while downing plastic cups full of cheap liquor, smoking cigarettes by the pack, and casually sneaking off to the bathroom to sniff lines of cocaine from the packs we had stuffed inside our cigarette boxes.

These house parties transformed into miniature raves. Drugs were everywhere, in the open. The air was heavy with the smell of cigarette smoke and weed. There was usually no furniture to be found, just an empty living room with a hardwood floor that served as a makeshift dance floor. Young men drifted in and out the house, coming and going with seemingly endless refills of drugs and booze. Meanwhile these kidz (these young gay boys who prided themselves on being flawless) would kick and fall to the floor as the beats banged from the speakers. These nights were endless, fluid, transcending from one level of sin to the next.

This was the environment JC and I thrived in. We feasted on sin, and I was an addict for him. I craved him. He was cool and sophisticated. He was stylish and popular. He was everything I wasn't. And so I followed him, this man, no, we walked together, hand in hand to the other side of sin, to the other side of drug use. By the time I found myself laying in bed hopeless and alone, desperate for a way out of the mess I had made I barely recalled how I had gotten there. All I knew was that it had taken a lifetime to find somebody to love and I didn't want to give that up.

I wanted to hold on to us, to him. I wanted to build something together but we didn't know how. I began to see that he wasn't capable of loving me, himself, or being loved in return for that matter. And so the question formed in my head: did I love myself? Would someone that truly loved their self continue to stay in a relationship with someone who was adding nothing of substance to their relationship, but instead chipping away at its frail foundation, seeming not to care about the consequences?

I thought I loved myself, hoped I had, but it was becoming clear that I didn't know what I was doing either. In some weird, perverted way I felt better than him, even though we were both doing the same things. I felt like I had to be more conscious than him...I had to be. I looked at him some days, looked into his eyes and listened to his dribbling and rambling words and I saw someone that was lost...lost and without a compass, and to me that was more frightening than anything else. He had no way out.

How had I allowed myself to fall in love with someone who could take me to end of the earth but didn't know how to get me back home?

I felt hoodwinked. I had played myself. I had been foolish enough to accept an imitation of love and somehow call it genuine.

I had been conned, taken in by this emotion and way of life that resembled love but was not the real thing. In fact, it had only drawn me further from the real thing...real love.

These revelations fell down on me like a shower of raindrops during the quiet of a storm. As my relationship with JC carried on it became ever so clear that I had trapped myself inside a hoax. It was all smoke and mirrors.

The truth was that I had no one to blame but myself. I had fallen for someone and into something that did not exist. I had fallen for a companionship that I had hoped for, prayed for, but sadly was not meant to be.

I was in that sad place where life makes no sense at all. Here I stood in love with a man, caring for him to the point of exhaustion, to the point that the pain he was causing me was beginning to leave me breathless. I had watched him, allowed him, better yet gave him permission to hurt me on more than one occasion, and the truth...the truth of the matter was that I secretly indulged in it just a little.

Sometimes the pain felt so bad that it was good and I didn't know why. The chaos and despair was feeding some crazy and twisted part of me that continued to call out for more. Like the time I organized his birthday party at a local bar. His friends all showed up and I brought along my aunt's famous spinach dip with Hawaiian bread. I, JC, and his friends all laughed and talked that night and had a grand ol time, and then it was time to go home. I packed everything up and we all began saying our goodbyes to one another. I assumed that my boyfriend, my supposed partner was going to come home with me, but instead he told me that he would catch up with me later.

I was stunned, to say the least. I thought to myself, "Didn't you say that you were mine? Didn't you say that to me—that you were mine?"

Had I had any sense of self-worth I would have raised hell, threw a fit, screamed and carried on, but I didn't. No, I asked for more of the same instead.

Like the time I had not heard from him in days and I drove around downtown Indianapolis searching for his car. I circled familiar streets where I thought he might be. I drove down alleyways, into parking lots, pass bars and bath houses thinking I might catch him there. Finally one night I saw his van sitting in the middle of the road on Walnut Street. This was the spot where hustlers prowled and waited on men to drive through who were looking for sex. We called this place "the beat." We would cruise this street after the bars let out, make new friends and meet up with old ones. It was our answer to social networking before we had Facebook.

As the months cooled down the crowd would fizzle. It had to have been late September or October when I discovered JC's van in the middle of the street because Walnut was almost empty then. There was no doubt in my mind that he had been on a drug binge the past few days and that was why I had not heard from him in so long. But now here he was.

As I pulled my car over I noticed him stumbling around the van, a cigarette dangling from his lips. I saw that the van had a flat tire. As I got out of my car and began walking closer I was prepared to help him change the tire. I wanted to get him and the van back on the road as soon as possible so we could argue about why he had stayed away for so long, ignored me, and then make up again.

I wanted to hear his lies and decide if I would accept them. Only as I was about to offer my help another young man came from around the side of a nearby building and began to approach us.

"He don't want your help, man" the young man came closer.

I put the pieces together quickly. This was either some hustler JC had picked up over the past few days or a drug-friend he must have had tucked away.

I hoped it was something else but it felt like heartache, betrayal. I was devastated. Was this the other man?

My heart was racing, time slowed down. I watched motionless, frozen as the two of them got the tire changed and I begged JC to go home. I begged him, do you hear me, begged him, cried out to him to do the right thing but he screamed back instead.

"Darvin, go home!" he told me.

I watched as the two of them got into the van and drove away. I limped to my car beaten on the inside. I picked up my cell phone and dialed, only to listen to endless rings on the other end. A lump grew in my throat and I pictured them going to a place I would never know. I imagined them in vivid detail...how they would get together, get high, have sex, and all the while listen to the phone I was calling vibrate against the hardwood floor.

The truth was clear. I was in a bona fide mess.

Now you would think that after all this I would have packed my bags, changed my number, something! But no. I indulged the insanity even more; played with the lunacy of my life as though it were made my Hasbro or Mattel. Instead of me doing something and making a wise, sound choice I toyed with my circumstances and used his foolishness as an excuse to indulge in my own.

I began snatching up other partners as well, two of them his close friends and the other a random stranger I met one night on the street. I came clean with him about what I had done, freely confessing my sins because I wanted him to suffer as much as I had.

I hoped that he would feel some sense of pain, just a piece of what I had gone through, only he didn't. In fact, he brushed it off very calmly, as if nothing had ever happened. He told me that if I could put up with him for so long surely he could put up with me.

I was too weak to leave him. I thought maybe he would see my transgressions as unforgivable and leave me instead, but he didn't.

I knew that it was over, but how do you say goodbye to something or someone that you loved for so long?

I fathomed the question for months. Our days became long and bizarre. Nothing was changing. In fact things were getting worse. I lost my job and fell behind on my car payments. I couldn't afford simple things like my cell phone bill. I was living with my grandmother, supposedly there to take care of her but I was the one who needed taking care of. I was drowning in my mess. My life felt like quicksand; every time I moved I sunk a little deeper. I was completely out of balance.

I buffered my pain with drugs, alcohol, and JC's company when I could get it. I wallowed in my self-pity and eventually I began to ponder the question, "What's it all for?"

What was the use in living anymore? What good was I doing? I had made a mess of everything in my life. Surely there was no hope for me.

I found myself pondering these questions onc night while lying in bed with him. I was drifting in and out of consciousness, in and out of crazy.

"If I was going to end my life, how would I do it?" I thought.

I was too afraid to use a gun and I would never have the guts to cut myself or inflict some sort of pain on my body. And it wasn't that I wanted to die, I just didn't know how to live any longer. So how could I do it? How could I allow myself a little more time but still know that this journey was going to end?

And there it was...my answer. I looked at JC and I realized that if we had unprotected sex I could catch HIV too, and maybe then I could speed up this agonizing process called life. I thought it over during the silence of the night and pondered what would happen if I did. My life flashed before my eyes, the good times and the bad times, and I thought of all the pain I would be causing other people. I thought of how stupid I was to even consider suicide when my life was not that bad, even though in that moment I did feel hopeless.

I took a breath. I didn't know what I was fighting for, but I realized in that moment, when no one else was looking, that life was still worth fighting for, and that was the moment I learned to say "Thank you."

Moments like these come to us like boulders in the road, forcing us to choose rather we want to live or die. And the truth is that sometimes there isn't much to thank God for (or at least that's how it seems).

Who would want to thank God for a burnt down house, an abusive husband, or children who seem to be testing you from every single angle? Who would want to thank God for an empty bank account or no food to eat? Who would want to thank God for any of that?

The truth is, however, that we're not always meant to thank God for all the things we can see, but for the things we can't see. We're thanking God with an expectant faith and believing that He knows more than us, can see further than us, and can deliver us into a future that we have yet to even dream of if we keep the right attitude. We trust that even though we've made all these bad choices and bad decisions that God still loves us, and God wants the best for us.

The Bible says "We are assured *and* know that [God being a partner in their labor] all things work together *and* are [fitting into a plan] for good to *and* for those who love God and are called according to [His] design and purpose," reads Romans 8:28.

I believe all God is looking for sometimes is a willing vessel, someone with the right attitude and enough faith and trust in Him to say "I don't know what this looks like, but I know that God's got my back and will never desert me of forsake me no matter what I think or feel around me!"

That is a radical attitude, and I believe that is what God is looking for– radical believers. He wants to see those who are trying to get to the heart of Him...Jehovah-Jireh–the Lord Who Provides, thank you.

REFLECTON QUESTIONS

Name all the things your thankful for; things worth living for.

CHAPTER FOUR

---

forgive yourself

No one wants to be vulnerable. We think of it as a sign of weakness. Most of us do everything in our power not to appear this way. We do our best to maintain this illusion of power, this illusion of control. We schedule our lives away on our iPads and smartphones, and we assume that by planning and organizing as much as we can that we can somehow stay ahead of the curve and therefore keep up this illusion of control.

We have our alarm clocks, biological clocks, and our internal clocks. We pride ourselves on not having time to waste, yet some of us are living on borrowed time. We steal time from things that matter most and give time to things that matter least of all. In the end we complain that we're out of time, have no downtime and God forbid something threw off our schedules because that would mean we wasted time.

All the religion in the world goes out the window the moment something goes wrong in our day. A lot of people don't have the patience to deal with change. The thought of doing something that was not planned or etched in stone freaks people out. But how many of us know that these moments of unpredictability are the exact moments the devil uses to hold us in bondage? The very moment you think you're in control is the moment the devil uses to control you. Nothing is set in stone. Bad things happen to good people, good things happen to bad people all the time. You may have worked for a company for years expecting to one day be promoted, only to be passed over for somebody that is less qualified, less productive, and cheaper to pay.

Times like these can leave you lightheaded; can make you feel like some type of failure when all you did was try to build something worth holding onto.

The devil will use any situation to keep you in bondage, so forgive yourself for all the things you did and did not do. Forgive yourself for not being the mother, father, daughter, grandmother, sister, brother, cousin, nephew, niece, or son, or anything else you could or would have been or done had the situation been any different. It wasn't and you didn't, so forgive yourself for the what if's of life. Free yourself with self-forgiveness. Stop condemning yourself on a daily basis.

The devil wants to bind you up in a spirit of confusion and frustration, a spirit of chaos and self-condemnation that prevents you from enjoying your life. He wants to use whatever he can to keep us from smiling. He will do whatever it takes to keep us shackled and to prevent us from praising God. He does whatever it takes to keep us from feeling worthy of who we truly are—children of God, worthy of love and acceptable in His sight.

We punish ourselves for not meeting our daily scripture quotas, and for not keeping our houses as clean as we had hoped for, somehow equating our self-worth with our time-management skills. We punish ourselves for falling in love with the wrong person, still forgetting that *all* things work for good for those who love the Lord and are the called.

The Bible says "For a righteous man falls seven times and rises again, but the wicked are overthrown by calamity," reads Proverbs 24:16.

We are meant to fail. We are meant to grow from these failures. Our falls from grace are no surprise to God, but an opportunity, a gift from Him, so that we might further develop the fruits of the spirit (love, joy, peace, patience, kindness, goodness, faithfulness, gentleness, and self control). And despite however it feels, or what it looks like, you were built to get back up again. You were meant to rise again and to grow in love.

None of this is possible, however, if we operate from a place of fear or self-condemnation. Many people fail to see the link between the two. Fear will breed self-condemnation. It will convince you that you are not pretty enough, smart enough, sexy enough, worthy enough, or good enough to get the things out of life that you had hoped for. And so we condemn ourselves (internally beat ourselves up, throw pity parties, exhaust ourselves emotionally) because we are afraid of what the end will be.

We become terrified of the what-if. What if I don't look good or what if I don't sound good? What if I don't make it or get the part or the job or the house or the car? What if they don't like me or they choose somebody else? What if I'm the one that's different or stands out? What if they tease me, or call me names? What if they talk about me behind my back, or better yet and even worse to my face. *What if I'm not worthy?*

This is the self-induced bondage of self-condemnation. There is nothing from God or of God in self-condemnation. If you have gone down the road of self-condemnation then you have surely gone too far. You need to make a u-turn and come back to reality. You have been tricked by the devil, and he has somehow convinced you that you are unworthy of a chance to fail or succeed. He has convinced you that you are unworthy of a chance.

This self-condemnation is not to be confused with the power of conviction. These are two different things. The Holy Spirit will convict us and cause a spiritual and moral unrest. This unrest is there to guide us toward enlightenment and to nurture us toward the fruits of the spirit. The devil, however, is there to condemn us and steal away our joy, our time, and our peace, leading us down a path that takes us away from the things that matter most and what we should be focused on.

Condemnation will take you captive and make you a prisoner inside your mind if you don't learn to forgive yourself for the mistakes you've made. We have to learn to stop pressuring ourselves with expectations we can't always live up to, promises we can't always keep. We have to accept that despite our attempts to be Christ-like we will never be Christ. We're going to make mistakes. We're going to slip. Things will not always go as planned.

Now I'm not saying you get a "Get out of jail free" card, but I am saying you need to learn to let go and let God. You don't have to keep beating yourself up as though it proves something, even though some people aren't happy unless you're miserable.

We have to learn to forgive ourselves for our mistakes, our flaws, and all the things we cannot change.

The Bible says "For You, O Lord, are good and ready to forgive [our trespasses, sending them away, letting them go completely and forever]; and You are abundant in mercy *and* loving-kindness to all those who call upon you," reads Psalms 86:5.

God is not sitting in heaven dwelling on what you did yesterday, ten years ago, last night, or even ten minutes ago. He's waiting on what you're going to do now. Have you learned from your mistakes? Did you grow? Are you more patient? Do you see the world differently? Did you get the lesson life was trying to teach you, or do you need to take the course over again?

Life is trying to teach you something. The question is rather or not you recognize what it is. For inside the lesson is the blessing. When you recognize what the lesson is you will find your breakthrough which will become your blessing. Everything else in life is just a symptom. All the pain, anxiety, and self-condemnation are all symptoms of your condition, there to grab your attention so that you may face the real issue.

What is the truth of the matter? What's it all about? After all the fear and self-condemnation, what does it all come down to? What are you not telling the truth about, and when do you plan on starting? That, my friend, is the question. What are you not telling the truth about? What are you not forgiving yourself for?

REFLECTION QUESTIONS

Is there anything in your life that you still haven't forgave yourself for? If so, was this something that was out of your control?

Do you think you could have changed the outcome if you had done something different?

Is there anyone's forgiveness that you're still waiting on and why?

What did you think would happen if things did not go as planned?

Did you learn anything in process, and do you think what you learned was the real lesson at hand, or do you still think there's more to it?

Have you been honest with yourself, or ignored the real issues?

What do you think the real issues are?

CHAPTER FIVE

---

embrace the pain

Most people do not enjoy pain, but the fact is pain still has great lessons to teach us. Like I mentioned before, when you accept the lesson life is trying to teach you, you will simultaneously accept the blessing God is trying to give you because the lesson *is* the blessing. This same principle can be applied to pain. Our troubles are there to teach us something, but for us to hear from the Holy Spirit we must be in a position to do so.

You will never hear the voice of God when you are fearful and living in negativity. These spirits will block out the voice of God. It is only when you live and walk in love that you are able to hear from God. This is the time when our spirits are most open to the possibility of what God is trying teach us.

So what was God trying to teach me the night JC came to my grandmother's house and woke me from my sleep? I have asked myself this question a hundred times.

It was late that night, about twelve-thirty. I had forced myself to lie down and had just fallen asleep when my cell phone rang. It was JC on the other end. He was on his way over. He sounded drunk and loud.

He arrived at my grandmother's house minutes later. I remember hearing the van he was driving come down the street, and I peeked through the blinds in my bedroom window and watched as he parked his father's white van in front of our house. My grandmother was in the room next to mine. Her door was open. She was still awake, sitting up in her bed, a water-spotted glass of Pepsi at her bedside—something to sip on throughout the night. I walked downstairs.

I imagined how our evening would go. I imagined that it would end like any other. He'd come over, we'd have some drinks, maybe do a little cocaine. I imagined we would talk for awhile; sit around my grandmother's dining room table and ramble on about nothing in particular. We'd say goodnight and he would drive back home. I'd go to sleep and wake up the next day just like any other.

With this in mind I threw on my blue Sean John sweatshirt and a pair of old jeans. I went downstairs, out the living room door, through the screened-in front porch and unlocked the security door and let him in. He was drunk as I had suspected and we went into the dining room just as I had imagined.

We sat down at the dining room table and began to talk. As it turned out he didn't have any drugs on him at all. I took a few sips of the drink he had in his plastic cup. I listened to him go on and on about how unhappy he was with his life. I could tell he was getting more worked up. Suddenly he told me he had to leave. He jumped up and told me to let him out. I tried to calm him down. I began begging him to stay the night. I asked him again, pleaded and begged him some more.

"Please stay. Don't go."

These were the words that were in my heart.

"I love you. I love you more, please stay."

But he refused. I followed him to the porch and we both stood at the front door. I didn't want him to go. I wanted him to stay the night. I missed him, loved him, was desperate for his attention, affection, and his companionship. I was desperate, you see, desperate.

Until now we had been one disappointment after the other, and I don't know why but I imagined that if he stayed the night things would be different in the morning. Maybe we could avoid *this* failure, this heartache, one less. But he told me "No." He wanted out in more ways than one. He screamed at me to let him out and so finally I did.

I relented, unlocked the door and stood back. We talked some more on the front steps. I followed him to the curb and then walked around to the driver's side door. I still attempted to lure him back in but then he shouted back at me "No!"

He slammed the door shut and I looked at him through the driver's side window. I began knocking on the glass and I watched as he turned the key in the ignition. I watched as he began to shift gears and put the van in drive. The wheels began to move and then it happened.

I felt a tug on the sleeve of my sweatshirt. I looked down, noticed that my shirt sleeve was caught in the driver's side door. I began screaming and banging louder.

"Stop! Stop driving! JC," I called. "My shirt is stuck!"

But he ignored me. Maybe he was too drunk to notice, or maybe he just couldn't hear me through the window. Perhaps he thought it was just another lame attempt of mine trying to get his attention, but it wasn't. It was a cry for help as I envisioned him dragging me down the street as if I were some slave hitched to a horse. I banged more and cried more but instead he went faster. I ran alongside the van as he sped up, but I was losing my footing, nearly tripping with every other step.

"He's going to kill me," I thought, "He's going to kill me."

I held on tight, gripping the door handle for dear life. I screamed; still, as I listened to the engine accelerate. The van sped off. The handle I was holding on to ripped away from the door simultaneously slamming me to the ground.

I fell to the ground face first, my front teeth biting the street as my head slammed against the asphalt. I lay motionless on the ground, dazed and amazed by the fact that I was still alive.

I peeled myself off the ground, looked down at my hands and saw bits of asphalt embedded in the palm of my hands. I could barely see. My glasses had flown off my face and were lost somewhere during the fall.

I stumbled to the house, up the steps and into the bathroom where I took that first look at myself. I was frightened by what I saw.

There was a wide red bruise down the middle of my face. One of my front teeth had been knocked out; the other crooked and pushed away from my gum. My arm was throbbing. My body was devastated. I tried to wash the asphalt from my hands. I lifted my pants legs and looked for any other cuts and bruises. I stood in front of the mirror gasping. What was I suppose to do?

I decided that my first step should be to get myself to a hospital. I picked up the phone and called JC, believing he would come back and drive me to the emergency room. But when I called no one answered. I could not imagine myself driving to the hospital alone and unable to see, so I drove to his house instead hoping he could take me from there.

I went to their side door and knocked. His mother answered. She was stunned by my appearance. I pleaded with her to let me see her son. I wanted him to see what he had done. And so I walked down the steps and into their basement and he saw me for the first time.

His mother played mediator and told me not to worry about anything. She said everything would be fine. She told me that she would take care of everything. She said that she would take care of all of my medical bills, even pay for my dentistry. As long as I went home everything would be okay.

I drove home, shaken but somewhat pacified. I believed her. Something in me was desperate to believe her. Somehow I had been deceived into thinking that this was all going to go away.

I took a bath that night and I remember the sting of the hot water as it trickled across my wounds. I took a few Tylenol and I laid down in bed somehow still thinking that I was going to wake up and this would all have been a dream.

But instead I awoke to a throbbing pain in my arm and I knew something was wrong. I became clear-headed enough to drive myself to the hospital to be checked out.

The admissions clerk looked at me in amazement. I wrote down my information and took a seat in the waiting room. The waiting room was quiet, calm, a sharp contrast to the chaos inside my mind.

A nurse called my name shortly after. They took me back to an exam room. They took x-rays and determined I had a fractured arm. I sat on the exam table inside the dimly lit room and waited as the thin layer of sanitary paper crunched underneath me. The nurses cleaned my wounds and used tweezers to pick out the asphalt fragments from my hands, and I cried as they asked me whether I wanted to press charges against JC for having done this to me. I told them "No" and I went home, battered but still in love.

When I came home I was in a fog. As I lay in bed the gravity of the situation began to kick in. I was broke, black, and foolishly in love.

I wanted my pain to mean something for JC. I wanted my pain to count for something. I wanted him to feel bad for what he had done. I wanted him to admit that he had screwed things up, and that he was in no condition to hold down a serious relationship. I wanted him to fight with me, for me, about me, for us. I wanted him to fight. I wanted him to care, but he didn't, not the way I wanted him to. Not in a way that made me feel better. My pain did not move him to action. I did not receive any bittersweet love songs or poems. For the most part nothing changed at all. For the next few days he called whenever I crossed his mind, visited whenever he felt like it and that was it. I felt as though I was burdening him with my misery.

Then one afternoon I found myself sitting at his kitchen table, my arm in a sling, hungry.

I had not been able to eat solid food since the accident, and I noticed a surplus of canned soup in his mother's pantry. I asked him for a can of soup as I was about to leave and he shot back "No! No you cannot have a can of soup. No, I do not want to give it to you!"

I was taken aback, flabbergasted. He was irritated by my circumstances. Perhaps he thought I was a burden. I was being too needy. I was absent-minded, foolishly thinking that this man was going to take care of me in my time of need. I was left breathless, stunned. I walked out of his house that afternoon without a tear in my eye. Instead I felt enraged, pissed off, angry at the fact that I had allowed this foolishness to go on for as long as it had.

I drove back to my grandmother's house fuming and contemplating how I was going to pull myself out of this situation, and so the true healing began.

I burned a sweater he had given me in the makeshift trash pit in my grandmother's backyard. I called him on the phone screaming venomous words, scolding him on his careless behavior. I told him I would get him back for everything he had done to me. I felt uplifted, energetic for the first time in months. I decided to be smart. I decided to start using the sense God gave me to make things better for myself.

I called a lawyer, made an appointment, and made plans to file suit against him for damages.

I informed JC of my plan to file suit against him and the insurance company. In a last-ditch effort to hold on to him I even told him that once the money came in we might be able to start over, but it was too late. They interpreted me retaining a lawyer as an act of war. I, on the other hand saw things differently.

I had been left with thousands of dollars in medical bills not to mention pending dentistry needs, and despite the promises his mother had made she had no intention of paying any of these bills. I was left to fend for myself. In an instant I lost partner and my friend.

What followed were days and weeks filled with misery and loneliness. I contemplated whether I had made the right choice. My lawyer took photos of my injuries. Things began to get real then. JC and his parents were served papers informing them of the pending lawsuit. I suddenly found myself free from JC's grasp, but I didn't want to be free. I was forced into it. I had no choice but to be free because he didn't want anything to do with me.

To add insult to injury my aunt came to me a week or two later and told me that she wanted me to move out of my grandmother's house. She was not satisfied with the job I was doing taking care of my grandmother. She told me I had two weeks to find a place and then it was time to go.

I called my mother who lived on the other side of town. I told her what I was going through and asked if I could stay with her until I figured out what else to do. She said yes. I called a friend to give me a ride to her house across town. I hid my car from the repo man inside my grandmother's garage. Everything I had held on to was gone.

I woke up every day just as tired as I was the night before. I was drinking from sun up to sun down. I hid bottles in the cushions of the couch in my mother's basement because I was ashamed of how much I was drinking.

My days became a blur, one day fading into the next. I didn't know how to cope with my emotions or how to acknowledge the pain and the loss of my relationship. I didn't know how to acknowledge anything. I just wanted to feel good and numb, and that's what drinking did. It took away the pain and offered me solace.

This was my way of grieving. My way of letting go was to not deal with things at all. I was afraid to move on, unsure of what lay before me. I was simply afraid to live.

But the truth is that God did not make us in His image only to leave us full of fear. God did not give us our test so that our testimonies would not be heard. God did not say "Now that you have endured all of this pain and suffering put your life on hold because you should be too afraid to do anything else."

The Bible says "If the son liberates you [makes you free men], then you are really *and* unquestionably free," reads John 8:36.

Most of the things we mourn are the things that never did us any good anyway, so why not celebrate our deliverance instead? Why not celebrate breaking free from the bondage of our past instead of grieving over the fact that we're no longer enslaved to it?

Most of us aren't as nervous about changing as we are irritated by how uncomfortable the experience is. We don't want to readjust ourselves. We are accustomed to slouching, holding our head down and dragging our feet in life. Now that God has come along and insisted that we might stand up straight, put our chins up and shoulders back we're not use it.

God is in the process of bringing us out of the wilderness and bringing us into the Promised Land, but some of us are dragging our feet every step of the way. We're screaming and kicking "No, no, no! I don't want to go!"

Meanwhile God is saying "I insist. I insist that you be blessed. You have lingered here too long."

We need to embrace the pain! Embrace it, breathe it in, take a big whiff of the discomfort and the sadness that abounds. Embrace the hurt. Embrace the shame. Embrace the heartache and understand that what lies behind us is already done, and that God will do a new thing. God is in the business of clearing away all the shame and despair that we bear. He's good at erasing the ridicule and the failures of our past. He is able to coddle you in his arms and place you down by still waters in a place of rest.

There are some promises that God has made to you that only you know, and His word cannot come back void. He is not a God that He should lie. All of the tests, trials and tribulations have not been in vain. The pain was not for nothing, but was there so you might know The One who delivered you. For all things work for good for those that love the Lord and are the called.

So let the pain of today be a reminder of the glory of tomorrow. Let the pain seep through and understand that God will get the glory somehow, someway, as long as you believe.

REFLECTION QUESTIONS

What's the most painful thing that has happened to you?

Were you able to push past the pain? If so, what type of life did you find was waiting for you on the other side of this pain?

If you were unable to move on, what stopped you?

CHAPTER SIX

---

simplify & downsize

I don't know about you but I spend entirely too much time focusing on other people. I find myself focused on things that have nothing to do with me, things that will never contribute to my life or my future whatsoever. Yet I keep going back to these same things, these same people and I don't know why.

I am trying to rationalize craziness. I sometimes fail to realize that craziness is a state of being, a disturbingly conscious awareness of one's irrationality and affection for a drama-filled life. It traps you in a cycle of addictive behavior, causing you to go back and invest time in those things that mean you no good. Now let me clarify. I'm not talking about those idle conversations we have on buses or at airports, but I am referring to the incessant gossip, the ongoing flirtations we give that beg for more of the same craziness. Do you hear what I'm saying? We give name, give place to these things and these people who mean us no harm, but mean us no good either. These are the people we keep around for sentimental reasons because they make us feel connected to a distorted reality that we have somehow grown comfortable enough in to call our own.

The truth is that I have come to know craziness all too well. I thought I could train but crazy trained me. I thought I could tame it and so I played with it and did everything I've warned you not to do.

A little crazy goes a long way. I say this because craziness can morph into something else. It can transform into something much more dangerous and much more life-altering than you may have imagined. This bit of crazy served up in just the right doses and at just the right time can transform into inner-chaos, a place of dismal unrest. Here we experience a yearning that is never satisfied because it yearns for the never-ending cycle of crazy that we sometimes feed ourselves, and so we suffer the angst of withdrawal.

Like many of you there have been days in my life when I have awoken with my heart racing, my mind full of anxiety. I try to shake it off, take deep breaths, pray and lay still until I can feel the hand of God cradle me, but the feeling can be relentless.

I close my eyes and picture a peaceful place of rest. The nights can be long, drawn out, spent tossing and turning until obligations pull me from my slumber, and I must go on just like you.

We push on through our day until it is done, until it is finished. We fall into our houses through our front doors weary from our days. And as exhausted as we may seem from the chaos of our night we are still compelled to stay connected to the craziness of our day. We log on and log in, text and tweet blurb after blurb until we collapse from exhaustion, only to wake up and do it all again the next day.

Like many of you I would wake up and say my morning prayer, "God help me. God save me. God protect me. God grant me favor," only to slide out of bed and check my cell phone for the latest gossip updates.

This is how I would start my day, with conversations and gossip of all kinds, improper and immoral conversations, feeding a growing anxiety that would eventually take my breath away.

This is my truth. I own it. I realized that I was my own worst enemy. I was hooked on chaos. I was hooked on foolishness, to the feeling of being connected to people twenty-four-seven because I was too afraid of being left alone, of being lonely. That was the real truth behind it all.

I was beginning to think I would always be alone. I began questioning this thing called homosexuality and whether or not the concept of having a life partner was even possible. The idea of being alone was catching up to me. I was afraid of it. I didn't want to spend time alone because I was afraid of what I would find within the silence.

I discovered that I really didn't like myself very much. I realized that I was a pro at beating myself up. Nobody could kick my butt like I could. I could torment myself internally and blame myself for every shortcoming to the point of fatigue. I practiced this for days. I abused myself mentally until I reached my quota of pain for the day. That's right, I had a quota. I could not continue on or enjoy life again until I had felt enough pain that I nearly drove myself crazy.

I hadn't truly learned to forgive myself yet. I knew I needed to, but a part of learning to forgive yourself meant that you casted your cares as quickly as possible, and I just wasn't there yet. Forgiving yourself meant that you were free from the weight of your transgressions, but I liked to carry mine around. It meant that you could make a mistake, feel bad about it but could still move on! That was it. There was no need to dwell on the past for years and years, beating yourself up all the while. No, forgiving yourself meant that it was done. It was over, finished, and even though you may have messed up you were still worthy of God's love and a good life. Forgiving yourself meant one's acceptance of one's worthiness of life, joy, peace, love, and rest.

I, however, had to learn the hard way. I was absorbed by feelings of inner-turmoil and inner-condemnation and so I lusted after the affection and approval of others. I was at such odds with myself that I looked outward for as much validation as I could get, gaining my sense of self from other people's opinions of me.

I fed off of people's compliments, their awe of me. I collected them, these people, these fans, and found my sense of worthiness through them.

I collected these people from the internet, from bars, nightclubs, not realizing that each of them had their own pre-existing conditions as well. I never considered that craziness is contagious, and that they could infect me with their own strain of venom. I put myself at risk by exposing my already sensitive condition to theirs and I paid for it dearly.

Time and time again I found myself panicked, nervous, and anxious because I had somehow sucked in all their negativity or perverted energy. I became a reflection of their distorted pasts and uncertain futures, their pains and their desires. I was infected by a condition of crazy.

The Bible says "Do not be in a hurry in the laying on of hands [giving the sanction of the church hastily in reinstating expelled offenders or in ordination in questionable cases], nor share *or* participate in another man's sins; keep yourself pure," reads I Timothy 5:22.

The Bible goes on to say "The sins of some men are conspicuous (openly evident to all eyes), going before them to the judgment [seat] *and* proclaiming their sentence in advance; but the sins of others appear later [following the offender to the bar of judgment and coming into view there]," reads I Timothy 5:24.

We know by this that everything is not what it seems. Every creature does not reveal its true nature at first sight, so we are told to be cautious of those things that we do not fully understand. That was my other problem. I was attaching myself to any and everybody without knowing what their intentions were, somehow thinking that I could outfox or outsmart them. I could sometimes feel that something or someone wasn't right but I kept them around anyway.

I thought that I was smart enough and discerning enough of the spirits around me that I could tell when it was time to go. I thought I had time to escape if something felt off, or strange, but the truth is that spirits shed and they imprint on our souls without us even knowing it. Spirits linger and impart on us, infecting us time and time again with negative energy or "bad vibes" until we are as sick as the company we keep.

That was why I would wake up breathing hard, full of anxiety and wondering what on earth was wrong with me. And so I decided that it was time to make a change. I decided that the time had come to re-evaluate my life, the choices I was making and how I was spending my time.

This desire for change was just the beginning of my being dealt with by God. He was preparing me for these changes by planting what I thought were random ideas in my head. These ideas lingered in my head. The possibilities clung to my spirit. I began contemplating a plan for peace. It was to be an itemized list of things I could eliminate from my life that would aid in bringing peace to my life.

The first thing I had to adjust was my internet usage. I found that I was addicted to porn and chat sites, any social media website that connected me to other people was a problem. Whether it was Facebook, Skype, or even Yahoo Messenger, I was hooked. I surrounded myself with their apps or websites all the time. Rather it was on the computer or my cell phone; it was a nonstop information highway, a volcano of confusion erupting in my life at all times.

Any attempt to answer the incessant amount of messages and texts, emails, and phone calls proved to be exhausting. It was a constant game of catch-up that became overwhelming.

Ask yourself how many hours a day you spend glued to your laptop, iPad, cell phone or Mac book. It's a never-ending cycle of information in a world where some of us would be better off if we just powered down.

And so God one day planted the concept inside my head, my heart. The instructions were simple: write down everything in your life that steals joy from your life and then attempt to get rid of it and look at the results after it's been eliminated. This idea seemed too simple and to overwhelming at the same time. How would I live without these things in my life? How would I survive if I didn't have all of these websites at my disposal? Nevertheless I went ahead and made a list of everything I could do to pursue peace in my life, and the plan for peace became very simple. First, I had to eliminate social networking sites—Facebook, chat sites, etc. Second, I had to begin meditating. I was in need of some quiet time badly; even it was just a minute or two a day. Third, I needed to get out of the house, live life in the sun, and enjoy nature more often. I had to stretch my legs and live life outside of my bedroom. Lastly, it was on my spirit to eliminate everything that had to do with homosexuality from my life. I had to stop chasing boys and going to the clubs if I wanted to achieve peace. Nothing good was going to come from that atmosphere.

That was it, four things that jumped out at me when I began contemplating my plan for peace. It was a literal pursuit of peace in my life, an aggressive action needed in a desperate situation. They were simple adjustments that could make a world of difference in my life.

Still the battle is long and hard. I became strong enough to eliminate Facebook from my life. I went weeks without touching other sites before breaking down and logging back in every now and then. The strength comes in phases. Some days are better than others, but I am reminded with every click of the mouse what craziness lies on the other side of the screen.

The fact is there is no way to have that many lines of communication open without being effected by them. People shed, remember that. Their spirits linger on. Their craziness becomes your craziness. Their laziness becomes your laziness. Their lunacy, their sexual immorality, their inclination to sin becomes your own. You might find yourself saying "What's the harm in a little this or that?" without realizing the sacrifices you're making in the meantime.

The damage is done in secret; the harm inflicted without your knowing, when you weren't looking. Careless living and wreck less association can steal your joy and your time. The danger is not that you'll rub off on them but that they will rub off on you. So what's the final word?

Well, naturally the final word is that you need to make your own list...your own plan for peace. Think about those things in your life that you know you need to let go or change. Ask yourself what's causing you to lose sleep, what's stealing your joy at night or waking you up in the morning. What things in your life can you feel infecting you with negativity? What does your spirit say? That was the key for me.

My spirit was trying desperately to get my attention but I ignored it every time. I knew deep down that I needed to be outside taking walks in the park but all this seemed so foreign to me, however, sin felt so familiar.

I knew that the party scene was infecting me with endless streams of boys and compliments, lies and gossip, drugs and alcohol. I knew that.

My spirit was speaking to me loud and clear, but like so many of you I was choosing not to listen. So ask yourself "What is my spirit trying to say?"

What is your spirit whispering to you? How is it trying to serve you? Pay attention and avail yourself of the gift one finds when living a more simplified and downsized life.

REFLECTION QUESTIONS

Name four things that take up too much time in your life. Now eliminate those things (or people) from your life for two weeks. In two weeks come back to this question and write down what your life experience has been like without having these things (people) in your life.

CHAPTER SEVEN

———

celebrate the grief

We all reach points in our lives when we feel that we are at our last...our last hope, our last cry, our last heartache. Sometimes it feels as though there is nothing worse in the world than withstanding the death of something or someone that you love.

One of the most difficult phases of healing from a broken relationship is the phase in which we find ourselves grieving for that which we have lost or given up. Some people use the term "really bad breakup" but the truth is that what we are actually experiencing is a feeling of grief over the end of our past life.

Grief is defined as a deep and poignant distress, often times caused by bereavement. It is the emotional and spiritual upheaval that takes us over during a time of loss, often accompanied by an often overwhelming amount of separation anxiety. Its symptoms include feelings of desperation, longing, loneliness and aloneness after we experience the loss of something or someone that has become familiar to us in one way or another.

I can remember the days after JC and I broke up. Our distance grew quickly as I explained why I hired a lawyer to sue him and his mother after they showed no interest in providing me with their insurance information. It was then that he decided to stop taking my calls and began treating me as though I were a stranger even though we had known each other for almost six years by then.

The truth was that he had never been any good for each other. Our entire relationship was built around our love for partying and drugs. Our time together almost always coincided with some sort of drug or alcohol use. Sober days were a rarity. It was a twisted romance but I loved him all the while.

That was it, I loved him. There was something about him that I couldn't do without. I desired his face, his time, his touch, his energy. I wanted to be near him, see him, craved him, hoped he wanted me too. I required something of him. His energy filled a space in me. I loved him in the mess and held his hand somehow thinking that I could save him from it without sacrificing myself in the meantime. But it was not meant to be. Sometimes that's just how life goes. Sometimes we fall for the wrong people, do the wrong things. Sometimes we find ourselves in relationships that we didn't necessarily ask for or need. No one asks to be abused or yelled at on a daily basis. No one asks for a relationship with a drug addict or an alcoholic. No one asks to be hurt. No one asks to be abused or misused but sometimes that's just what happens, and despite our knowing or being told that we need to leave sometimes we stay anyway. Because that's what humans do. We act on emotion, martyr our spirits, and cast rationality aside in the name of love.

We stay knowing that our spirit is saying "Get out."

We stay for what looks like too long. Some of us escape though, only to look back and wonder how we made it through and why we couldn't stay longer.

A lot of us desire the pain. We desire the hurt, the shame, and the despair because anything else feels out of

Stop Feeding Crazy & Pursue Peace

place. We don't know how to handle things or people that might be good for us because we are so accustomed to being treated so wrong.

We have to learn how to receive what God has waiting for us on the other side of all that heartache and pain. We have to learn how to grieve but not to get stuck there.

I wanted to die after breaking up with JC. I felt lifeless. I couldn't recognize myself. I didn't know how to smile, how to eat. Numb. I had to learn how to laugh again when someone has betrayed you. I had to learn. But God...

Surely we all have the ability to pull ourselves out of the pit of grief we dig for ourselves and back to a meaningful and spirit-led life. We have the ability to utilize the power invested in us by the Father to call upon his name and to fight back with the word of God in moments when we feel we just can't take anymore.

The Bible says "Therefore also now, says the Lord, turn *and* keep on coming to Me with all your heart, with fasting, with weeping, and with mourning [until every hindrance is removed and the broken fellowship is restored]," reads Joel 2:12.

God did not say "Now that you are at this impasse in your life give up on everything that you know and hold dear."

No, the Lord said "I want you to turn and keep on coming!"

Turn away from that foolishness that you are crying over. Turn away from everything you think you wanted in life. Turn away from the pain and the shame that you use to know. He's saying that if it's broken he'll help you fix it, but you have to come to Him.

However, the road to a relationship with God can be tricky. Inevitably what seems to happen is that in the midst of our turning away from our past something or someone comes along to distract us from what we should be focused on, which is our future with God. This causes some of us to look back on our past with a longing heart instead of turning toward God.

If you keep looking to the past you will stay in the past. In Genesis, chapter nineteen we read the story of Sodom and Gomorrah...The story of a man named Lot who was shown favor by two angels who had come to destroy the city of Sodom because it had become morally detestable to God.

Lot invited the angels in, tried to protect them from the others in the city who wanted to seize them, and in return they showed him favor and allowed him to leave the city.

They told him to take his son-in-laws and his daughters and to run to the mountains far away, or else he too would be overtaken by the destruction as well. Lot told his son-in-laws and his daughters but none of them moved quickly, so eventually the angels had to carry them out of the city. The angels went on to tell Lot and his family to flee to the mountains, but Lot rejected the idea.

"Surely not the mountains," he protested. "What about the city of Zoar?"

And so the angels relented.

"You may go to Zoar," said the angels. "When you arrive we will destroy the city."

And so Lot and his family began to travel to Zoar and finally they arrived. The heavens began to rain down fire and the city of Sodom was destroyed. And then the Bible goes on to say that Lot's wife looked back and instantly became a pillar of salt, reads Genesis 19: 1-26.

Most people like to illustrate how Lot's wife was turned into a pillar of salt because she looked back, but I feel like we've all heard this story a million times. What stands out to me more than anything in this story is the line **"And when they had brought them forth, they said, Escape for your life! Do not look behind you or stop anywhere in the valley; escape to the Mountains [of Moab], lest you be consumed," reads Genesis 19:17.**

The word consumed illustrates that there is a chance of them being overtaken by their past if they do not keep their focus on things ahead.

The Bible says "So if the Son liberates you [makes you free men], then you are really *and* unquestionably free," reads John 8:36.

But what so often happens is that God grants us an opportunity to escape our situation, opens a window in our lives for us to flee a person or a thing that has held us down and inevitably some of us freeze. We take two steps away from the very thing that has caused us grief and anguish and we buckle under the grief. We don't want to go through the pain of letting go and the emotions of moving on. We don't want to be uncomfortable. We don't want to embrace the pain and celebrate the grief, no; we want to go back to what we know instead.

Some of us have to learn to catch the vision. We have to learn that no matter how much we think we know we don't know much at all. We have to learn to let go and to let God.

The truth is that most of us are grieving situations because we have tried to force the hand of something or someone outside of God's appointed season. How many of us are guilty of trying to make something happen? How many of us are in relationships that should have ended after date number one or two, but instead we allowed them to become long-term relationships that God never said "Yes" to in the first place. We have tried to run things our way but the results are often times disastrous.

I was in a relationship– my first real relationship with a young man, and we lived together for about four years. By the end of our relationship we had lived together in three different apartments, had bought a couple cars together...The Lord had blessed us to both make more money on our jobs; we took vacations and little weekend getaways...We maintained a very traditional relationship even though we were two men living together in what I then called sin.

We liked each other enough to make it work. I cooked, we both cleaned, we both did the laundry. It was a very normal relationship for the most part, but there was still something tugging at my heart.

I began to feel exhausted and drained. I did not feel like my usual self, whoever that was at that point. I found that I had made concessions for and because of someone for so long that I did not know who I was or what I wanted anymore.

I knew it was time to get out. I knew it was time to bring this rollercoaster to an end.

I had been consistently reading or hearing the word of God for about a year. I didn't know it then but the power of God's word was doing something in my life. Every sermon or message that I heard, every word that I read was strengthening me to become the man God had intended me to be. The only problem was that the new man and the old life could not coincide. They just didn't fit.

God was doing a new thing in me, and that old foolishness that I was holding on to had to go.

The relationship I had, the one I had complained about for years had to go. I was being pulled in a new direction. I was being strengthened and set free to do a new work, this work...

The truth is that sometimes God has to pull you from what you thought you wanted to take you where you *need* to be. He may also allow you to stay in that place of pain just so you will know it was Him who brought you out.

The Bible says "Behold, all you [enemies of your own selves] who attempt to kindle your own fires [and work out your own plans of salvation], who surround *and* gird yourselves with momentary sparks, darts, *and* firebrands that you set aflame!—walk by the light of your self-made fire and of

the sparks that you have kindled [for yourself, if you will]! But this shall you have from my hand: you shall lie down in grief *and* in torment," reads Isaiah 50:11.

The Bible is very clear that when we work outside the will of God there is a price to pay, and that price will ultimately result in grief. But know this: we serve a merciful God and He has shown us that He will transform this very same grief into a blessing that we cannot imagine.

Your grief may look like the end of something but it is actually the beginning of something new. It is the beginning of something great, something wonderful that you could not have imagined until now.

God wants us to know who's in charge. He wants us to know that He is the only one who can truly bring you out of bondage, but you have to be open to the possibilities.

You have to be open to the fact that victories don't always look like victories. They don't always look like what you wanted. The grief is not only there to remind you of a pending victory but to remind you of the pending possibility of a new day.

Your life opens up when something dies. It becomes a blank canvas. It becomes fertile ground for something new, but you have to be willing to first plant the seed of change. You have to be willing to open yourself up to new ideas and new ways of doing things. You can't be closed off or you'll miss the blessing.

The truth is that blessings come in all different shapes and sizes, but you'll never know the sweet smell of success or the joy victory if you don't allow yourself the gift of possibilities; only then will they become endless.

REFLECTION QUESTIONS

What do you miss about the past life you had?

Do you think you will ever have this again? If not, why?

Do you feel worthy of what it is you're asking for?

CHAPTER EIGHT

---

stop feeding crazy

The truth is that crazy is always calling. Crazy is like a stray cat that won't leave your door because you keep feeding it. Crazy is calling to us from every angle, every crevice, and every altitude. It's out there in the shape of crazy ex-boyfriends and girlfriends, lovers who should never have been lovers, people who do their best to pick at you until there's nothing left. Crazy is the club you keep going to that's draining your pockets and leaving you hung over the next morning. Crazy is you not paying your tithes but wondering why nothing seems to go your way. Crazy is you disrespecting your mother and wondering why your own kids don't respect you. Crazy is you shopping for things you can't afford but wondering why you're still broke. Crazy is you waking up with an attitude and talking to people as if *they're* crazy. Crazy is talking down to your children and wondering why they have low self-esteem. Crazy is you beating up a woman when you say that you're man. Crazy is you needing a better job but not willing to do what it takes to get one. Crazy is you believing the voice in your head that says you're not good enough. Crazy is you not cleaning your house and wondering why people talk about you. Crazy is you knowing what to do but still choosing not to.

It's crazy to think that you're going to take everyone with you on this journey called life. Everybody is not meant to go everywhere. They're not all meant to take your journey with you. They won't all make it. They're not designed to. They're not like you. They won't all get the big picture, nor will they all understand what you mean when you say God has given you a vision. They won't all see with the spirit. They won't all see through your eyes or eyes of love. They won't all understand what being a child of God means. They won't all understand what it means to have a calling on your life. They won't all get it and that is nothing to be mad about.

The Bible says "And if your right hand serves as a trap to ensnare you *or* is an occasion for you to stumble *and* sin, cut it off and cast it from you. It is better that you lose one of your members than your entire body should be cast into hell (Gehenna)," reads Matthew 5:30.

We are told to cut off those things which offend God and our spirits. We are told to pursue happiness and peace. We are told to do the best we can with what we've got, and in the meantime not to beat ourselves up over the things that we cannot change; for this change will come in time too.

Of course some of us still compromise who God has called us to be in favor of things that are easy and carefree, but this too is a part of life. Mistakes and wrong turns are meant to be; for they are what promote growth in us. They are what shape us. They are what bend the branch that forms the tree and gives it character. They are what make us who we are, and there is no shame in making them, but there is fault when we turn from wisdom on purpose.

So this too must be considered a way of life- how we play with fire and dare it not to be cool.

We test life. We pick at it, poke at it like its some rodent laying motionless by the side of the road that might show its teeth and bear down on us. We take chances, sometimes good and sometimes bad. We return to things that mean us no good.

The Bible says "So a dog returns to his vomit, so a fool returns to his folly," reads Proverbs 26:11.

A lot of us are going right back to what we've been running from expecting a different result. If you didn't like it then there is a good chance you won't like it now. If it bothered you then it might bother you now...until them, it, or you grows. And when that happens you'll know.

The Bible says "When I was a child, I talked like a child, I thought like a child, I reasoned like a child; now that I have become a man, I am done with childish ways *and* have put them aside," reads I Corinthians 13:11.

What can I say to make you reconsider your thinking? What metaphor can I give to impress upon you the importance of living your life in a different way? Stop feeding crazy. Stop going places you know mean you no good. Stop surrounding yourself with people you know aren't going anywhere in life. Just stop. Stop crying over some man or woman as if they were the only person in the world that will love you.

Stop feeling sorry for yourself when you know that something better, bigger, and brighter is waiting for you on the other side. Stop feeding crazy and grow up. Get over the fact that a dead relationship has come to an end. Stop feeding crazy and get over the fact that a job you hated has let you go. Stop feeding crazy. You're better than this and you know it. Stop stooping to a level you never belonged on in the first place. Stop lowering your standards. Stop coming down to their level when you are so much better than that. Get over yourself and grow up. Can't you see that God is trying to bless you? He's trying to give you something, but He can't give you this blessing unless He separates you from the things and the people that are attempting to hold you down.

71

Life is meant for the living, for those not afraid to bear a little persecution, a little shame, a little condemnation, a little suffering.

The Bible says "Therefore, those who are ill-treated *and* suffer in accordance with God's will must do right and commit their souls [in charge as a deposit] to the One Who created [then] and will never fail [them], reads I Peter 4:19.

Another version reads "So if you are suffering in a manner that pleases God, keep on doing what is right, and trust your lives to the God who created you, for he will never fail you," reads the New Living Translation.

I want you to understand what I am saying. I want you to process the fact that we need to stop playing around. We will never grow up and walk into the destiny that God has planned for us if we do not stop playing around.

God's change doesn't always feel good, and I know that walking away from something that you've loved is a hard thing to do...because it's what you've known. I get it. Change hurts. It stresses you out. It leaves you stunned and breathless and wondering what on earth you'll do now that your sky has fallen or has turned gray. However, if we can manage to stop feeding crazy, to stop pursuing those things which we know aren't meant for us our lives could change. We could change the world because we would finally be in a position to possess our greatness. We could reign, you see, as kings, the one inside us. We could claim our place on this earth. We could claim our skin, our breath, our time. We could live life as though we meant it, you see...if we stopped feeding crazy and acted like we knew who we were, are, am, to be, you see. Stop feeding crazy.

REFLECTION QUESTIONS

When did crazy call out to you and did you know it was really crazy?

Do you think you ignored the warning signs, and did you think it possible to change it into something good?

CHAPTER NINE

---

the truth about joy

Your joy is your weapon against the devil. It is your most basic, most overlooked, most recommended, most necessary weapon in life. It is a derivative of pain, prayer, fasting, meditation, solace, and faith. It is a product of all those things combined. You get saved, you read your word, you begin to pray, fast, and seek God's face and you begin to experience the joy of the Lord. You begin to wake up happy and gleeful, beaming with energy and hope because you are experiencing the joy of the Lord (as we like to call it).

Your relationship with Him begins to grow and evolve and you begin to learn things and suddenly you are experiencing this profound sense of peace and nirvana. You find that joy is an emotion you feel because now things are possible that were not possible before. Even in bad times you find the possibility of change, of recovery. There is the possibility of something new, something better, something different. There is the possibility of hope, and that, my friend, is the truth about joy—it is all about the possibility.

We bask in the light of this possibility until inevitably something or someone comes along with bad news or the inconveniences of life and suddenly we find our joy meter dwindles down. You might find yourself wondering what on earth has happened to all that joy you had a couple days ago. You don't know where it went or what happened, but you know it disappeared and you know you want it back.

This is what happens every day to people all around the world. It is what happened to you, to me, and will happen again in the future. It is a cycle, life. You live, you learn, you hope you do better in the future.

All of us are constantly fighting for joy. We constantly make our way back to it, finding that the path has changed every time. We take it for granted. We treat it haphazardly. We cry when it's gone and overlook it when it's there.

But what are we looking for?

Joy is defined as the emotion evoked by well-being, success or good fortune or by the prospect of possessing what one desires. Another definition describes it as a state of happiness or felicity, or bliss.

It is different from happiness because happiness is usually based on what is happening. It is contingent on the moment, on what is going on. Joy, however, is based on what could happen, the possibilities of a new day.

Say for instance you have gotten married, gotten a big promotion at work, just bought your dream house or a new car, the emotion you experience will probably be happiness. Now flip the coin over. Let's say there's nothing extraordinarily exciting happening in your life but there's nothing extraordinarily wrong with it either. Let's just say you're going through the motions. You wake up every day, go to work, raise the kids, and cook the meals. You do everything you're supposed to do but you can't feel joy.

There have been days in my life when I have felt this same way...when I have rationalized gratitude but not been able to feel joy.

We are so often told the things which we should be thankful for as if thanks equals joy. The truth, however, is that they are two different things.

It is highly possible for somebody to feel thankful and have no peace, but there is no peace without joy. These two things feed on each other. They are inter-woven, intrinsically connected, festering without the strength of the other. They rely on one other, grow with one other, and nurture one another.

Joy is fed by peace. Without joy you are likely to feel as though your peace is impossible to find because the other truth about joy is this: joy is hope. It is hope in the possible, hope in the unknown, the unseen...The hope that feeds faith and says "Yes, it will be okay."

When someone says "I can't find my joy" what they are really saying is "I can't find my hope" and that is the truth about joy. So the question becomes *how do I get it back?*

The Bible says "But the fruit of the [Holy] Spirit [the work which His presence within accomplishes] is love, joy (gladness), peace, patience (an even temper, forbearance), kindness, goodness (benevolence), faithfulness, Gentleness (meekness, humility), self-control (self-restraint, continence). Against such things there is no law [that can bring a charge], reads Galatians 5:24 and 25.

So we know now that what we must do is seek the Holy Spirit, seek God, and lean on Him for understanding. That's the only way you get your joy once your hope is gone.

I can tell you now that I know what it's like to lay in bed tossing and turning at night. I know what it's like to plead the blood of Jesus in those hours of the night, when all hope seems to be gone. But I also know what it's like to come out on the other side after you've done the work.

You've got to pull yourself out of the rut you're in by seeking God's face and asking guidance. And I'm not saying that God will mysteriously appear before you in a cloud of smoke with this great answer to all your troubles. But you do need to exert the energy into the universe that signals to other life forces around you that you need help. Change will come when you ask for it.

When you begin to exert energy into the world in the name of change things will happen. Life will rise to meet you when you rise above it.

Secondly, you've got to lay off all the other stuff—the men, the women, the drugs, the alcohol, the foolishness that confines you to the life that you've lived without joy.

Third, you've got to clean your plate. Stop looking at the situation as if it were the end of the earth. Try to look at it as an opportunity to correct whatever issues you've had in the past.

Fourth, some of us need to get out into the world and get busy living instead of wasting time withering away. We need to take advantage of this beautiful gift called life.

Some of us have been in a daze for so long we can't see our way out. Still, I am here to say that the day has come. Today is your day. You're going to live. You're going to make it.

Now that doesn't mean all things will magically happen and change, but it does mean that you can get your joy back. You can get your hope back.

The Bible says "The thief comes only in order to steal, kill and destroy. I came that they may have *and* enjoy life, and have it in abundance (to the full, till it overflows)," reads John 10:10.

The devil has come to separate you from every good thing. He has come to make your life one of misery if you're not careful. He does not want you to know the fullness and the rest found in God. He wants you joyless, bound up, and of no benefit to the Kingdom of God—the kingdom that strengthens each other, other people, promoting love, wisdom, peace, change, and hope in God.

He wants you removed from the possibilities. He wants you distracted, caught off guard, kept busy and hidden from the work you should be doing.

The Bible says that the devil is a thief. A thief is defined as one that steals especially stealthily, or secretly. Another definition describes a thief as a person who steals another person's property. The fact is your joy is your property. You earned it. It's been bought and paid for and I think someone out there needs to get a little angry that the devil is trying to take it away!

Your joy is your weapon. Understand this. Without joy you lose your fight. Amen? You lose your energy, hope, the get-up that gets you moving. Don't let the devil take what's yours. Don't let him con you into thinking that you have to give up your joy because you've come out of something, from someone or somewhere that did you no good.

Broken relationships and brokenness has the ability to steal your joy. It's that simple. I could spend the rest of my life crying over the way JC treated me following my injuries. I could wallow in the fact that he offered no condolences at all.

Of course I was devastated by what had happened. I could not believe that my life had unraveled the way it had.

I spent days on end in my mother's basement, numbing myself with alcohol until I found myself in a drunken fog. I hid liquor bottles in the cushions of the sofa because I did not want anyone to know how much I was drinking. I was ashamed of myself, but that's just what Satan does. He convinces you through condemnation that you aren't worth anything. He tells you things, whispers deceitful lies in your ear so you think you're the only one who's ever felt that way. He makes you feel unworthy, as though you were some sort of failure. But what we must remember, especially in times when our relationships are being tested is that people are in your life for a specific season and a specific reason. Some people will say that they are here for one or the other, but I believe they are here for both. I believe that God is continually pruning us, teaching us lessons so we will be better equipped to do His work.

Jesus said "I AM the True Vine, and My Father is the Vinedresser. Any branch in Me that does not bear fruit [that stops bearing] He cuts away (trims off, takes away); and He cleanses *and* repeatedly prunes every branch that continues to bear fruit, to make it bear more *and* richer *and* more excellent fruit," reads John 15:1 and 2.

We know by this that God is in the fruit-bearing business. Whatever is not good will be plucked away until we can bear richer and more excellent fruit, and sometimes what is plucked away is a relationship that was just getting in the way.

People don't always mean to harm you. It would be easy for me to have built up hatred in my heart when JC denied me a can a soup even though he was the one responsible for knocking my teeth out. It would have been easy for me to build up hatred for my next boyfriend when he jumped on my back causing me to fall down and break my arm. It would have been easy for me to hate them both.

Hatred does not take much work. It is one of the most natural things to do. It's an easy emotion. To dislike someone doesn't take much thought or much energy, but to love somebody despite of their wrong doings, to forgive somebody once they have done you wrong is something completely different. It takes character, grace, faith, hope. Love takes time. Love takes patience. Love takes energy, thought, and compassion.

The Bible says "Love endures long *and* is patient and kind; love never is envious *nor* boils over with jealousy, is not boastful *or* vainglorious, does not display itself haughtily. It is not conceited (arrogant and inflated with pride); it is not rude (unmannerly) *and* does not act unbecomingly. Love (God's love in us) does not insist on its own rights *or* its own way *for* it is not self-seeking; it is not touchy *or* fretful *or* resentful; it takes no account of the evil done to it [it pays no attention to a suffered wrong]. It does not rejoice at injustice *and* unrighteousness, but rejoices when right *and* truth prevail. Love bears up under anything *and* everything that comes, is ever ready to believe the best of every person, its hopes are fadeless under all circumstances, and it endures everything [without weakening]. Love never fails [never fades out or becomes obsolete or comes to an end]. As for prophecy (the gift of interpreting the divine will and purpose), it will be fulfilled *and* pass away; as for tongues, they will be destroyed and cease; as for knowledge, it will pass away [it will lose its value and be superseded by truth]," reads I Corinthians 13: 4-8.

Love never fails but sometimes people do. People are flawed and they make mistakes. They hurt other people even though they don't always mean to. People are imperfect and they make bad decisions and stupid choices, often times not realizing the consequences their actions will have on other people. But they also suffer just as you do. Hurt people hurt people, but love conquers all. It can surpass hate and bring you to a place of peace, a place of possibility.

The Bible says "If you keep My commandments [if you continue to obey My instructions], you will abide in My love *and* live on in it, just as I have obeyed My Father's commandments and live on His love. I have told you these things, that My joy *and* delight may be in you, and that your joy *and* gladness may be of full measure *and* complete *and* overflowing. This is My commandment; that you love one another [just] as I have loved you. No one has greater love [no one has shown stronger affection] than to lay down (give up) his own life for his friend. You are My friends if you keep on doing the things which I command you to do. I do not call you servants (slaves) any longer, for the servant does not know what his master is doing (working out). But I have called you My friends, because I have made known to you everything that I have heard from My Father. [I have revealed to you everything that I have learned from Him.] You have now chosen Me, but I have chosen you and I have appointed you [I have planted you], that you might go and bear fruit *and* keep on bearing, and that your fruit may be lasting [that it may remain, abide], so that whatever you ask the Father in My Name [as presenting all that I AM], He may give it to you. This is what I command you: that you love another," reads John 15:10-17.

Love hard and press on is what Jesus is telling us to do. Don't beat yourself up because something went wrong. Don't continue to hate someone or something because of what they didn't do. Don't waste your time being frustrated resenting something that you can't change. Do what you can with today; figure out what you can do with today. Don't let the devil trick you into thinking that you won't always win with love because you will! Love will bring you into a place of peace, a place of rest, a place of joy if we continue to faint not, and press on in the name of love, in the name of God, and in the name of possibilities. Your hope is your joy. Don't let him take that away. Press on in love.

REFLECTION QUESTIONS

Name five things that bring you joy (or use to) and then go do them. Go for a walk, take a long bath, take a picture of something you find beautiful. Take a deep breath and let it out, and then do it again until you feel a layer of stress melt away from your being. Learn to breathe again.

CHAPTER TEN

---

praise your way through

I know what it's like to be stuck in the wilderness. I know what it's like to want to be more than what you are. I know what it's like to want to be somebody that does great things but no one gives you a chance to do them. I know what it's like to look inside yourself and see someone the world may never get a chance to see because you are too preoccupied with feeding crazy.

You see crazy can show up in more ways than one. It can manifest itself in a fluid-like way. Like energy, it can be neither created nor destroyed. It simply changes form from one thing to another; come to attack you in various ways whenever possible. It is often unimaginable, seemingly unrelenting and yet consistently self-inflicted. Crazy can distract you from what you are meant to be doing. It can come in the shape of a boyfriend, supposed best friend, the club scene, or substance abuse.

It could be gambling, overeating, or the inability to say "No" because you feel as though you're going to miss something if you don't accept every invitation possible.

The sad part is that most of us can recognize crazy from a million miles away, yet we still dive into it, all the while saying, "Man....This is crazy!"

We know all the "ought not's" of life. We know all the people we ought not hang out with, the foods we ought not eat, the places we ought not go, calls we ought not make, and the risks we ought not take, but we still do.

We take the risks and the calls, keep the company and eat the foods, all the while hoping that we won't suffer the consequences. We pray that the consequence will pass us by, hoping that we are somehow above reproach. We think to ourselves, "Crazy will never catch up to me. Anyway, what's the worst that could happen?"

For some reason we think we can tame crazy, wear it down and turn it into something manageable. We think we can flirt with it, wink our eyes at it, and expect to leave unscathed.

Most of us have come out of these situations kept only by the grace of God. Most of us are where we are today because God put a fence around us, protected us from the harms and dangers of the world that we sought purposely. Most of us have mingled, fraternized, shacked up, and laid down with more life-altering and life-ending situations than we will ever know. There are things that could have happened, would have killed us, should have infected us had it not been for God's grace. Nevertheless, we still find ourselves in the wilderness.

We didn't realize that as we were flirting with temptation the devil was actually leading us to a place of darkness, to a place of lost dreams and coulda, woulda, shouldas.

This place is called disconnect. It is a place of unrest. It is a place where the weary get no sleep. It is a place full of crazy, things that make no sense, bubbling over with every opportunistic distraction one can imagine. The devil likes to keep us there. He likes to trap us in crazy, amused by how we go around in circles as we make our way through the wilderness, only to find ourselves right back where we started, having made no headway, and just as lost as before. You see crazy is here to detain you from the vision God has given you, the destiny God has put on your life, the victories that are waiting for you on the other side of crazy. Crazy has come to hold you up. That foolishness that you have been dabbling in and playing with is nothing more than a distraction for you, a way of preventing you from achieving the success you were meant to achieve. But I have come to tell you that the time has come to press on past crazy, past foolishness, past distractions, and past all the other games that you have been playing to a place of peace, a place of rest and victory, a place of real love.

Now there are many examples of people continuing on with foolish and unwise behaviors throughout the Bible, but one of the greatest examples of being totally caught up in craziness is found in the book of Exodus. Here we find the story of how the Israelites were brought out of bondage from Egypt and journeyed through the wilderness toward the Promised Land for forty years! One would think that God would have expedited their journey because they were His chosen people, but this was not the case. Not only did God not lead them into the Promised Land quickly, He saw to it that they took the long way home, the long way to victory.

The Bible says "When Pharaoh let the people go, God led them not by the way of the land of the Philistines, although that was nearer; for God said, Lest the people change their purpose when they see war and return to Egypt. But God led the people around by the way of the wilderness toward the Red Sea. And the Israelites went up marshaled [in ranks] out of the land of Egypt," reads Exodus 13:17-18.

God said "If I take you the short route, the fastest route, you might not learn everything I'm trying to teach you because you may become afraid of what you see along the way."

God has to teach us things so that we will comprehend them. He can't always take us down the easy path in life because we might miss the important things along the way. He often times takes us down the path less traveled so we will recognize what He is trying to teach us along the way.

Now the word wilderness simply means a tract or region uncultivated and uninhabited by human beings; an area essentially undisturbed by human activity together with its naturally developed community; an empty or pathless area or region. The wilderness is simply uncharted territory. In other words it is a part of your life that has yet to be developed, so when you find yourself in the wilderness try to understand that you are simply traveling in uncharted territory. What you're going through has yet to be analyzed. There is no plan or course of action for the time you spend in the wilderness because you have never been there and have no experience to draw from. It's brand new, like a baby brought home from the hospital, daring you to ask "What do I do now?"

However, we're not talking about what to do once you're out of the wilderness; we're talking about what to do when you're *in* the wilderness and trying to find your way out. You see the foreign lands of our lives are there for a purpose. The wilderness is there to teach us things about ourselves, to prune things away from us, to reveal pieces of ourselves that need to be worked on that we may not know existed.

The wilderness is there to strengthen us even though it may look as though God has abandoned us. It's all in the way you look at it; the power of perception.

The Bible says "Death and life are in the power of the tongue, and they who indulge in it shall eat the fruit of it [for death or life]," reads Proverbs 18:21.

The Israelites kept saying they were lost and so they were. They kept saying Moses didn't know where he was going and so he didn't. But did they ever say "Thank you?" No.

And so they were lost and lingered and struggled to make sense of it all...their journey. It was all about their attitude. The key to their victory was is in their perception.

You see when you look at the Israelites and what they went through you will find that it wasn't their sense of direction that kept them from entering the Promised Land, it was their attitude. Time and time again God proved himself to the Israelites. He protected them. He made manna fall from Heaven. He kept them for forty years. He even commanded Moses to meet with Him on Mount Sinai where he gave Moses specific instructions for the Israelites, but when God didn't move as fast as the people wanted they revolted.

The Bible says that "When the people saw that Moses delayed to come down from the mountain, [they] gathered together to Aaron, and said to him, Up, make us gods to go before us; as for this Moses, the man who brought us up out of the land of Egypt, we do not know what has become of him," reads Exodus 32:1.

The fact is most of us are guilty of the same thing in our own lives. When God doesn't move as fast as we want we get restless. We decide and make up our own minds what God should be doing and when He should be doing it. This leads to haphazard choices.

We say our situations are hopeless and after time they become so. We say our situations are joyless and soon this manifest as well. We are speaking our lives into existence by putting out words of discouragement that eventually come back to haunt us. It's all in the attitude. The secret to victory, however, is praise. Praise your way through no matter what it is you're going through.

You see the Israelites praised God in the beginning, after their exodus from Egypt. They sang and they danced and they shouted how mighty the Lord was until He began to take them through the wilderness. It was at this point that their praise began to grow dull and the murmuring took over. Praise was the secret weapon no one was investing in.

Praise is your weapon against the devil. Praise is your number one defense when the devil has your back against the wall and you don't know what to do. Praise will hold you, keep you, protect you during the moments when you think you're about to lose your mind. Praise will pull you through.

The truth is the devil will try to trap you in your own mind with the seed of condemnation. He will tell you lies, whisper to you that you're not good enough, that you'll never make it, and that you're not worthy to enter into heaven. He will tell you that you are too disgusting and too vile to be of any use, but the truth is your price has already been paid by Jesus Christ.

He will attempt to convince you that you are the lowliest creature on earth, a nobody, meant to do nothing but live in misery, but I am here to tell you that the devil is a liar and that praise *will* pull you through!

When you find yourself in the Wilderness of Sin and you don't know what else to do just start praising Him. When you think you're at your last, just about to lose your mind just start praising Him.

The Bible says that "From the first day of the seventh month they began to offer burnt offerings to the Lord, but the foundation of the temple of the Lord was not yet laid," reads Ezra 3:6.

Still the Israelites continued to give money and the people struggled to build the altar and then it says **"And when the builders laid the foundation of the temple of the Lord, the priests stood in their vestments with trumpets, and the Levite sons of Asaph with their cymbals, to praise the Lord, after the order of David king of Israel," reads Ezra 3:11.**

You see David knew the importance of praise, and so he ordered the people to praise God because the foundation had been laid. It was the start of something new, something different, something big. It meant that their days of offering sacrifices on dirt floors were coming to an end. It meant that the temple was on the way. It meant that the foundation had been laid for a brighter day.

Some of us need to realize that the time to praise God isn't when the work's all done, but when it's just beginning; when it's the most difficult and when it's the hardest.

Don't think that you have to praise God at the end. You can praise God for the foundation. Praise him for being able to pay off one credit card, or being able to make a single payment at all.

Maybe your refrigerator isn't full of food, but praise God that you have one to fill. Praise God for the foundation of something good.

Maybe you didn't get the car you wanted, but praise God for the one you have, or for the bus you ride. Maybe you're living in your parent's house, and you beat yourself up because you don't have your own...praise Him for the foundation anyway. You have a home, somewhere to lay your head, even for one more day. There's a foundation. There's something to build on. Praise Him for the little things, the bits and pieces. Praise Him for the ability to take baby steps toward victory. Pull yourself up with praise. Do ya hear me? Praise your way through.

REFLECTION QUESTIONS

Cut the TV off and the cell put the cell phone on vibrate and just take a moment to praise God for all little things, the big things, and everything you need to.

CHAPTER ELEVEN

---

surrender

"Who am I?" This question drives the human condition. It drives and pushes you toward what will become the rest of your life.

We ask ourselves "How do I fit into this world, this planet, this space, this time? How is my energy connected to your energy? How do my words affect your words and your wellbeing? Does my purpose mean anything to you? Is my being here, on this planet of any value to you? Am I an inconvenience to you? Does my presence mean anything to you? Do I matter at all? *Who am I?*"

You see what makes this question different and separates it from all other questions is that this question is unrelenting. It has the ability to follow you all the days of your life, often times becoming stronger and louder as the years go by. This question lingers in the spirit and grows into more questions like "How do I fit into this world? Do I have roots? Who are my people? Where is my home? Where do I belong and then who to?"

This question isn't like all that others that float in your head. No, this question demands an answer...an answer that you as a human being are hard-wired to acquire.

You have no choice but to heed to these questions because it is a fundamental part of the human condition to want to know how you fit in. When you don't "fit in" you may feel weak, isolated, and not equal to those around you. You may feel like an outcast, the new kid in school that sticks out because no one knows them yet. You may feel alone, scared, and uncomfortable which often leads to bad choices as we attempt to make up for our so-called inadequacies. Yet beyond these inadequacies is a life of freedom if we just learn to surrender.

You see when you don't know who you are you go out of your way to create an identity for yourself. People tend to latch onto whatever or whoever is close by and convenient for them to deal with when they don't have roots of their own.

Life is hard for those without a sense of self, a sense of place; and so we carve out niches for ourselves in *and* where we feel most comfortable. Be it sex, drugs, food, or alcohol, it doesn't matter what it is as long as it gives you a sense of power in your times of weakness.

The sad part, however, is that where we fit in is not necessarily where we need to be. Our seeds have a way of drifting and sometimes land in places where they were never meant to be.

There is a chance you were not meant to be in the garden you're in. There is also a chance that where you landed was where you chose to go, not where God chose to put you.

"But what's wrong with that?" you ask. "What's wrong with building a life somewhere you feel comfortable? Isn't that what life is all about...building a life that fits *your* needs."

And yet the answer often tortures us. Everything is not for everybody. What looks good to you may not be good for you.

You may not realize it but you may be exerting more force and more energy than your situation really requires. You may be exerting more energy than is necessary to stay in a situation you were never designed for. So what do we say about this? What is the remedy for seeds that have gone astray? Well it's simple; we need to grow where we are planted.

If I take a cactus and place it in Aspen it will freeze. If I take a Douglas Fir and plant it in the desert it won't survive. You might be a beautiful jambu tree whose roots should be in Indonesia, but if I uproot you and place you in Michigan you will surely die from the frigid temperatures.

Every time you decide to uproot yourself and go against the will of God you place yourself in a boxing ring with God, and who do you think will win?

You are not meant to wither and die. You are meant to blossom and bear fruit but you will never accomplish this if you are not willing to grow where you are planted.

"But how do I grow where I am planted?"

The answer is simple: surrender.

You have to surrender to God's will. You have to put aside what you want and allow yourself to be open to the possibility of something new, something different, something else. You have to put aside what you want in favor of what God would have you do, and until you do you are withholding blessings from your life.

One of the greatest examples of surrendering can be found in Jesus himself.

The Bible says "And He came out and went, as was His habit, to the Mount of Olives, and the disciples followed Him. And when He came to the place, He said to them, Pray that you may not [at all] enter into temptation. And He withdrew from them about a stone's throw and knelt down and prayed. Saying, Father, if You are willing, remove this cup from Me; yet not My will, but [always] Yours be done. And there appeared to Him an angel from heaven, strengthening

Him in spirit. And being in agony [of mind], He prayed [all the] more earnestly *and* intently, and His sweat became like great clots of blood dropping down upon the ground. And when He got up from prayer, He came to the disciples and found them sleeping from grief. And He said to them, Why do you sleep? Get up and pray that you may not enter [at all] into temptation. And while He was still speaking, behold, there came a crowd, and the man called Judas, one of the Twelve [apostles], was going before [leading] them. He drew near to Jesus to kiss Him. But Jesus said to him Judas! Would you betray *and* deliver me up the Son of Man with a kiss? And when those who were around Him saw what was about to happen, they said, Lord, shall we strike with sword? And one of them struck the bond servant of high priest and cut off his ear, the right one. But Jesus said, Permit them to go so far [as to seize Me]. And He touched the little [insignificant] ear and healed him," reads Luke 22:39-51.

Jesus decided to grow where he was planted. He made decided to stop fighting. He decided to surrender. He had a destiny, a purpose to fulfill. There was a plan for His life and His death. There was an end in store; a goal that had to be accomplished. And even though it wasn't going to feel good there was a reward on the other side; for on the third day He rose with all power in his hands. The work was done. The torture, the stoning, the mockery was over. He had all power and glory, but first He had to surrender. But what do most of us do?

We fall in line with the apostles. We become stricken by our grief. We become exhausted by our sorrows. We give in to the woes and rest with our misery.

But what would Jesus say do?

Jesus said to the apostles "Pray that you may not [at all] enter into temptation."

Jesus knew the cost of sorrow. He knew the cost of wallowing in your tears and in your fears. He knew that if you wallow too long you will give into temptation; for temptation is our remedy for sorrow.

And how so?

Sorrow is a deceiver. It tells you, convinces you that you deserve a reward for your suffering and your pain. It tells you that you should make yourself feel good...you should do something outrageous, silly, or something out of the ordinary for all the grief you have endured. Sorrow is an excuse to mess up. It is an excuse to do wrong, to make bad choices, to make bad decisions. It is an excuse to abandon the life that sustains you, to risk it all on one night of pleasure, one night of passion. It is an excuse to entertain the sins of the world, the temptations that lurk at your window, prowling and calling you by name. It is an excuse to lay down with the devil and let him feed you all the lies you can take so that you can go even deeper into temptation. It is a place many of us know all too well, some of us never to return from again.

And how do we come to this place of sorrow? How do we get to this place of pain, this place of exhaustion, this place of siege?

For many of us it happens in the moments when we're not looking, when we're not paying any attention. It is during these moments that we tend to let our guard down, not intentionally, just haphazardly. It is during these times that we tend to get caught up in the moment. We begin moving too fast, doing too much, going too many places, making too many commitments, and before you know it there it is—a day when you're weak, not prayed-up, and not thinking straight. You may find that you haven't read your Bible in a week or two, maybe you haven't gone to church in a month, and you're not sure how it happened, but it did. You may begin to feel foggy and out of focus. Your brain may seem a little fuzzy. You're not thinking straight. You can barely see straight. You're blood pressure is high. You're walking funny. You're talking funny. You can't think, can't move. You may find that you're exhausted and you don't know why. The doctors say it's depression but your spirit says it's something else. You don't know how it happened but you know no pill will fix this. You need God. You can feel it. This is a God issue, a spirit issue, and there's only one remedy in times like these. You need the Word and you need to surrender because time is running out.

This is when it happens—the fatigue caused by entertaining the devil. When you don't study, when you get out of your routine of prayer and spending time with God these moments become the ones he uses against you. He begins to whisper to you, lies to you, means you no good. In fact, he has come to kill you; for he is a deceiver, a robber, a thief, a heartbreaker, a joy-stealer, betrayer, an enemy never to be forgotten, on the loose going to and fro seeking that which he can devour. He is there waiting for you at every turn and every bend. That is why you must be prayed-up, studied-up, worshipped-up and anointed-up.

When you are not filled with the Word of God it becomes easy for the devil to deceive you.

I can tell you firsthand that I have witnessed his attempts on my life, and I know that had it not been for God I could never have made it through. I can tell you that there have been days when I have heard the voice of the devil in my head saying "Who do you think you are? What do you think you're doing? Who do you think you're talking to? Who is going to believe you? You're a phony, a loser, a pretender! You will never be anything. You're trying to make something out of a do-nothing life. Why don't you just kill yourself and die? Do us all a favor and just get it over with already. Just die!"

And some days I have thought, "Maybe I should...Maybe I should just end it all. Maybe that's the answer to all this...death."

And then, thanks be to God I hear a voice, a quiet voice saying "I will not die but live and will proclaim what the

Lord has done. Though you have chastened me severely You have not given me over to death."

However, if I did not have the Word of God in my life none of this would have been possible. I could have fallen for that garbage and those lies. I could have easily sunken into my sorrows and fed on those lies just like people do every day.

You want to know why people kill themselves: they become exhausted from their sorrows. They become weary and think that they don't have the strength to make it anymore.

Living takes courage. It takes determination. It takes guts...to see if you have what it takes to make it through one more day...To see if you have what it takes to make it through this journey to the end.

Our hearts become burdened, ambushed by the devil's lies. This is why we must pray to make it through just one more day. Just one more day...

You see when the devil whispers those things in your ears you're giving him room to walk into your life. When you fail to pray and study it begins to affect you in a serious way. You will feel the change. You will notice things in your life aren't the way you left them. You will notice things don't feel right in your spirit. Your spirit man becomes weakened and is often screaming out to you "There's something wrong here! There's something out of sorts here! You have to do something now!"

You know when it's not right. You know when you've been affected. You know what you must do to change it. You have to surrender.

By not surrendering you sacrifice your joy and your peace because you're pushing...pushing for something to happen.

We stop trusting. We stop believing. We stop feeling like we're making progress because everyday doesn't feel like sunshine. There isn't some miracle waiting for us every morning. It isn't how you thought it would be.

Christianity and spirituality don't always feel practical. Some days you don't *feel* like spending time with God or worshipping God. Some days you don't feel like being bothered. In fact, you don't always feel overjoyed from being a Christian, and that's nothing to be ashamed of. You're just human.

We don't always feel saved. A lot of us still feel like something is lacking or missing. All of us want to know who we are but it doesn't always become clear as fast as we want it to.

You see the issue with sorrow and what makes it so alarming is that it creates a vicious cycle. One bad choice leads to another bad choice. One bad move leads to another bad move. If you have a bad day you might give yourself permission to go out and do something foolish and stupid, and then you wake up the next morning beating yourself up for what you did the night before. And then what happens? You begin to meditate on your bad choices and you go even deeper into your sorrow and so you decide to do something else to make yourself feel better, and the cycle continues on and on and on. This is a cycle of sorrow, a cycle of self-pity where you and I play duo roles as both the culprit and the victim.

What we need to do is create a cycle of success. We need to revise and update our negative self-talk with the Word of God. We need to speak hope in times of despair and encourage ourselves even when nobody else wants to. And even if you don't have an encouraging word you at least need to muster the strength to say "Jesus, help me. Whatever I'm in, help me. Pull me out of this cycle of sorrow and despair. Just help me. Help me, Jesus..."

There's no more time for playing the victim.

The Bible says "For a righteous man falls seven times and rises again, but the wicked are overthrown by calamity," reads Proverbs 24:16.

You've got to get up, no matter what the situation looks like. It doesn't matter who or what died or went wrong, you've got to get back up. No matter who left, or how long they said they'd be gone you've got to pick yourself back up. Slowly and maybe with baby steps, you've got to get up. You have to do it for yourself as well as those who need you to tell them "*You* can make it."

I have seen sick people, friends and family of mine who struggle with illness, whether it be HIV, cancer, or just the common cold, and I have noticed a common thread between them. You see I have noticed that the physical fight is accompanied by a simultaneous mental battle. People fight not only the physical illness but the battle inside their minds that says "Can you or can't you make it one more day?"

Some get weary; some get tired, some succeed and some pass away, but no matter what the battle is we are all faced with a choice. We can decide to do it our way or to do it God's way. We can decide to lift our issues up to God, or we can struggle to figure it out for ourselves, hoping for the best.

We can decide to do away with the pressure of having to figure it all out, and to accept the fact that what will be will be, and when I have done all that I can there is nothing left to do but stand in the face of God. I can stand and rest in His will, His peace, His space, His time.

This does not mean make a fool of ourselves by rushing to every possible solution we can, only to cause more confusion in the process. But it does mean that when you have done everything you can do, everything that fits into God's will, and there is nothing left to do by all means surrender.

That's what it all comes down to. Once you've done what you can, what God says, or what He wants, there's nothing left to do but surrender. And sometimes your all ends up being nothing. Your all could mean stillness. You simply do the best you can with what you've got and you let it go. That's right, let it go. Just surrender.

REFLECTION QUESTIONS

What are you still trying to hold on to?

What excuses do you give yourself to do foolish things?

What is your self-talk when you fall short of your goals?

Does this self-talk feed your spirit or kill it even more?

Do you give yourself permission to be human or beat yourself up for not being God?

CHAPTER TWELVE

---

be available to change

A lot of us, right now, are living lies. We walk around, hold down jobs, kiss men and pretend to love women. We wonder if they love us or like us back, or are they living a lie too, holding on to an illusion that many of us call reality.

We are looking for answers to questions that sprout up inside us like dandelions after a hard rain; seeking wholeness in a world full of uncertainty.

How can it be that the yellow brick road of life has turned so crooked and so jagged? How can it be that some of the people in our lives we thought were there to love us only hurt us instead?

It seems that we taught ourselves to play it safe, make do with things and people we assumed would never hurt us. Some of us prepared ourselves for a life that would give us just enough but never more. And so these lives, as safe as they may have been have become our traps. They have become cages of suffering, quiet anxiety, and uninspired hell. They have become dungeons, battles of spirit with no sign of a victor. They quietly collect the best of us as we deny ourselves true authenticity.

The truth is that in these moments of unrest what you're really going through is the agony of change. It is the agony of transformation from one being to another, from one level to another, from one victory to another. And the truth is that change hurts. It causes pain and heartache and can make you uncomfortable. It causes you to sit up at night and wonder what on earth you've gotten yourself into. It broods and causes you to wonder "Who am I? How did I get here?" and "Where am I going?"

You see change is the act of transforming from one being to another; to make radically different.

As Christians we believe our change is used for a different purpose, a greater good. We believe our change is intended to make us more Christ-like, more amplified, more in the image of love. We believe we are meant to become the promise of the possibility, the person only you have seen inside the crevices of your mind.

You are meant to be the victor. The devil knows this and this is why he fights so hard against you. This is why he keeps you up at night, wakes you up early, causes you to get no sleep. It's an attempt to steal your joy, to distract you from your purpose, and to ultimately kill you if you allow him to.

How then do we fight back? How do we confront these demons that call out to us from the corners of our minds, that lurk in the creeks of hardwood floors reminding us that we are not alone? How do we confront the winds that blow, the craziness that stirs the nest we've built for ourselves. How do we stop feeding crazy?

Well we do it by confronting the lie and showing it the truth. We do it by growing a little backbone and finally calling a spade a spade. We do it by looking at the issues, the frauds and lies and calling them what they are—deceptions.

We are required to say so. Be it a bad marriage, a bad relationship, boyfriend or girlfriend, a bad job or investment deal...We are required to say so. We are required to confront the issues and go through it. How else will you ever grow up and beyond what you fear unless you tell the truth about what it is? How else are you to move on if you never face your fears head-on?

There is nothing more debilitating and confining in life than pretending to be something that you are not.

You cannot benefit anyone by living a lie, least of all yourself. In fact, most people have already seen past your facade they just haven't told you yet.

You see the only thing that holds us back in life is fear...fear of life, truth, reality. Yet you will find that if you are able to conquer these fears and embrace this change the life you are fearful of may just be one that can bring you joy.

For example, I use to be afraid of ducks. Every time I saw one I became terrified. My heart would skip a beat if I came close to one. All of this from one bad experience.

You see I was barbecuing one day in back of my apartment and a swarm of ducks and mallards were nearby. I saw them watching me and thought nothing of them when suddenly one flew directly at me as I was cooking.

I dropped the lid on the barbecue pit and ran inside. I slammed the door shut and watched in fear as this duck held my food hostage. I waited for them to leave before I went out again. The memory of this fear persisted until the Lord began telling me that I needed to go outside and begin communing with nature. Only then did things change.

It took me months to build up the courage and the nerve to be obedient to His voice.

Finally, one day I bundled-up my coat, put on my hat and pushed in my ear buds. I took off walking and eventually I arrived at a small flock of ducks and mallards gathered together by the side of the lake by my apartment building. I felt my heart race as I scurried past them, and as I did so I became flushed and hot with anxiety and fear. But in the midst of my fear I noticed something. I noticed that as I went near them they waddled away and fled back to the water. And so by the third day of walking past these ducks I realized that they were just as afraid of me as I was of them. I realized I had let the actions of one speak for them all. They weren't all bad.

I realized that I wasn't afraid anymore. In fact, the next time I saw a duck I took its picture so I could remember what God had done.

That is what you must do with fear. You must tackle it head-on, address it, and accept that change is nothing to be afraid of.

So what am I saying? I'm saying that our task in life is to become conscious of fear and to speak truth to lies.

I look at my life and I see areas where the truth was revealed to me and it was up to me to become either changed or unchanged by what that truth was. You see I told you that the truth is that I am a sinner, one who has done everything they were big and bad enough to do. In fact some of you might say my sin is one of the worst kinds because I identify myself as homosexual. But is one sin any greater than another if it is indeed a sin at all?

You see I was never one of those undercover brothas who attempted to hide themselves behind words like "discreet" or "down low." I was never one to hide behind lies, no. I was on the search for truth.

And so this search led me to questions like "Where did this sin come from," and "Why am I being punished for it? Why would I be sent to hell for something I had no control over...as if somebody can simply turn off their sexuality."

It was an assault on my senses, an insult to my spirit, and an attack on my person. Why had I been made this way and pre-destined for hell? Why was my salvation not enough? Who did this to me? What for and how come? And so my search began.

I reverted mentally and I found myself facing another duck; another fear that had to be faced.

I went back to a place that I had pushed down inside me because I was afraid of what I would find there. I went back to some of the first moments I had ever contemplated being with a man.

I thought back to my childhood, a little boy I knew in the third grade I once dared to hump the floor when nobody was looking. I thought back to the little boy who lived next door to us I once tried to take advantage of. But there was something else.

I searched back through my mind and the caverns of my brain where secrets can be found, and there it was...a garden of secrets.

You see a seed had been planted in me. It had blossomed into a garden of secrets and lies, its branches casting shadows in my world. Questions stood catty-corner to lies; my field spotted with dirty little saplings whose roots dug deep into my grass.

I was being poisoned by these lies, these secrets, infested in a way that had left me numb to the effect of its consequences. I had been poisoned by a memory that I had suppressed for years and now it was bearing down teeth, ready to devour my world.

The pain of this poison ignited memories in my head, flashes of a time once forgotten.

I thought back to when I lived in Michigan with my father and stepmother at the end of my third grade year. My parents had hired a babysitter to watch us that summer. He lived in the adjoining building with his mother. His name was Tremaine. He was seventeen, a high school senior. He was funny, cool, attractive. He didn't care what we did as long as we were having fun.

I remember we ordered pizza one afternoon. The box was white with red and green letters on it. Noble Romans, I think. I remember the sun coming in through the slits of the vertical blinds and cascading across the floor. I remember my stepsister was in one of the bedrooms taking a nap. He and I were in the living room sitting on the floor in front of the brown couch with the ugly pattern on it. I remember him putting a VHS tape in the VCR and waiting for the movie to start. Finally the movie opens with a man and a woman lying on a blanket outside under a tree. They begin to kiss and touch each other. They begin to do things, sexual things to and on top of each other. I don't know what to do so I just sit there shocked, stunned, bewildered, and unaware of the pending transgression to come.

Tremaine is next to me and I remember vaguely, like patches of memory and time that do not want to be acknowledged that his hands are touching my hands. His pants are loose, unfastened. He is doing something, showing me something, himself. He is aroused. My brain stops and won't open itself up to a memory that is too hard to bear. I know it is wrong but what is worse is that I like it.

I am aroused, titillated, and yet revolted and ashamed. This becomes my greatest fear, my greatest curse; a transgression that will follow me all the days of my life.

I hope that the secret will somehow disappear as if it was a dream, but it doesn't. Instead the seed grows and blossoms into my tree of secrets, stretching its branches the span of my life, infecting me with the shame, the secret, and the question that will never be answered—if I had not met this boy would I be gay? The truth is that we will never know.

From then on I lived out this curiosity until I no longer had to hide it. I embraced the gay lifestyle. I was no longer wondering what it was; now it had flesh. I could touch it, taste it, kick it, breathe it, hold it, love it, hate it, fear it, and let it in until it gave me what I wanted—incomplete satisfaction. Be it joyful or pain-filled the life was mine to have. Only now I wondered if the life I was living was just the result of one vexed afternoon spent with a named boy Tremaine.

I dove into the lifestyle head-first and eyes wide open. I wanted it all. I wanted to feel the tingle, the heat, and the energy of it all. I wanted to know what the songs were about; those that spoke of love and heartache, pain and suffering, good times and bad times, freedom and bondage, penance and sacrifice. I gave my all, all the while despising the constant self-judgment and wounds of paranoia while still thriving on the thrill of the unknown. It was my sustenance.

I only wanted what every other twenty-something hopes for: a love that feels like something...something real, something good, something like what dreams are made of. I wanted to experience the wrath of the fairytale. I wanted to feel the joy of love and taste the salt of tears against my lips. Only I wouldn't mind at all because it would be for love, after all; a love and a life worth fighting for.

I wanted the whirlwind romance but what I got was life instead. Ups and downs, bitter and sweet, nights that felt like heaven busting loose and hell breaking open. I got real life, the unabridged version like we all do at one time or another, and then I got complacent.

After JC and I broke up I found a relationship I thought I wanted but this too came to an end. I felt the anointing on my life telling me that there was something more for me to do, something greater than sitting in my apartment watching the world go by. The time had come to move, and *that* is what God is telling some of you to do. The time has come to move and to set a new course, you see.

I prayed, like many of you, for a day of strength, a day of deliverance, a day of change so I could push past my complacency. I prayed for a day of motivation and then one day it came...The day I had waited for.

I asked myself "Is this relationship forever?" and the answer was "No."

This affair was not meant to last a lifetime. It was not meant to *be* my life. I was strong enough to see the truth.

Truth, you see, is what most of us hide from. We want to keep living in the fantasy, the lie, the land of half-truths. We live on unspoken words that we twist into sought-after validation. We hope no one will call our bluff or notice our lack of authenticity yet God does. He notices and is calling to us to change.

Change, you see, does not always start with a giant leap, but sometimes begins with a crawl as we acknowledge our truth bit by bit until our destiny is revealed.

The Bible says "A time will come, however, indeed it is already here, when the true (genuine) worshippers will worship the Father in spirit and in truth (reality); for the Father is seeking just such people as these as His worshippers," reads John 4:24.

And that is what real changes comes down to: truth. The truth about your husband, your wife, your children, your parents, your coworkers.

The change you have been hoping for is not impossible, but is already here. However, you must be available to the truth in order for you to find the change you've been looking for. Change will come, you see. When you accept the truth it will come. So what is the truth about your situation? That is the question.

REFLECTION QUESTIONS

Are you making yourself available to change or are you living in a world of fear?

What are all the things you would do if nothing were stopping you?

CHAPTER THIRTEEN

---

accept your greatness

Why do people downplay their greatness? Why do we deal with people and do things that we know are beneath us? Why do we insist on being content with mediocrity when the skin that we're in was meant for so much more?

I have come to realize that we have failed to find the greatness within. We have failed to accept the fact that we were made in the image of God, The One, The Beginning, the End, The All.

Some of us have failed to look within. We are lost and waiting but we don't know what for, and so procrastination devours this thing called time which in the end is the stuff that life is made of.

What matters most is not the validation we seek from others whose opinions have become paramount in our lives. Still we look to them for the lessons that we should be teaching. We fail others by not educating their minds and liberating them from these fear-based doctrines.

We fail each other by holding our tongues and speaking these half-truths, afraid of what the whole truth will do. It seems that few possess the courage to shine the light of hope on another. We hold in our praise and words of wisdom, fearful that another person's light might outshine our own. Oh, but here is my truth...

The truth is that mediocrity, good enough, and "might as well" attitudes have become a refuge for millions. The art of getting by has overtaken the minds and spirits of those around us, and so we are left to contend with a world that is lacking vision.

The Bible says "Where there is no vision [no redemptive revelation of God], the people perish; but he who keeps the law [of God, which includes that of man]—blessed (happy, fortunate, and enviable) is he," reads Proverbs 29:18.

People give up because they have no vision. They have nothing to push them on, nothing to reach for. God gives us visions so that we might be motivated. Only then is our faith forced to grow and stretch; all for the purpose of a vision.

You see a vision is defined as something seen in a dream, a trance, or ecstasy; a supernatural appearance that conveys a revelation. A vision is described as a manifestation to the senses of something immaterial, something that has not happened but is yet to come.

That is God's promise to us—unspoken covenants between God and His children called visions.

But all visions are not the same. You see a mirage is a type of vision too. It can appear to look like a tangible object but as you get closer you realize it doesn't exist at all. It is an optical illusion, a visual effect...a game player's play.

You see a mirage will have you thinking that what's in front of you is a gift from God when in fact it is a set-up orchestrated by the devil himself. This is especially true when you are outside of the will of God.

When you do not accept your greatness you are likely to fall for anything. We mistake material possessions for authentic lives, pawning off our truth and replacing it with greedy ambition and a gluttonous yearning to be a part of the who's-who of the world.

So many of us are overtaken by a desire to obtain more, consumed by an illusion that only uplifts the flesh. Yet the flesh is never satisfied. It will feed an illusion until it expands, broadens, grows, and finally becomes a nightmare.

The search for this mirage may lead you down a road of destruction and despair. We may find ourselves disappointed and heartbroken and asking ourselves "Why?"

"Why did this happen to me? How did I not see this coming? How could I have been so stupid?"

We beat ourselves up. We find ourselves disappointed and heartbroken as we reflect on all the time, money, and energy wasted on something that was never meant to be.

But be ye encouraged; for you are not alone, nor will you be the first or last person to make a mistake.

Illusions can be beautiful, but what we must remember is that God's visions draw us closer to Him; while a mirage pushes us further into a world full of good intentions and hopes still differed.

God gives visions because He has something He wants us to do, learn, fight for, or engage in. He wants us to rise to the occasion. He wants to see you grow and learn as you proceed along this journey. He wants to see your heart expand until it has reached its fullest capacity for love. Love, the end result and what it all comes down to...what we are meant for, created for, meant to embody until our flesh cannot withstand anymore and we are called upon to leave this earthly plain.

Hear me now and understand that the vision is meant to encourage you and meant to pull you closer to this fundamental Godly principle for all things involving mankind.

Visions can be burdensome, tiring, and heavy because they often weigh more than we think we can bear. Great visions can appear to be vast and unobtainable, but this is only because great visions require greatness.

The vision requires you to live up to your full potential, to strive for something you never thought was possible. They dare you to reach for what some call the impossible. They dare you to reach for greatness. They ask that you accept the call on your life and not compromise or run from the truth that is within you. They dare you to embrace a legacy of faith wholeheartedly. You see it is only when you accept the vision that you can accept the possibility of your greatness.

The vision has come so that you might be raised up to that which you are. The vision has come so that you might fulfill your destiny of greatness.

The Bible says "And I, Daniel, alone saw the vision [of this heavenly being], for the men who were with me did not see the vision, but a great trembling fell upon them so that they fled to hide themselves," reads "Daniel 10:7.

You might be the only one that can see your vision. Others are not required to see what you see. They may laugh, joke, and call you names behind your back. But you be encouraged. They do not need to understand why you do the things you do. They are not required to have a clear understanding of the vision God has given you for your life.

It is during these times that others may fall away, just like the men that were surrounding Daniel.

These men did not comprehend the circumstances surrounding Daniel, but they could still feel that change was coming. It was this shift in their senses that made them fall away due to a fear of the unknown.

Something was happening and they did not know what or why, but they knew they could not withstand the level of greatness required for the task at hand. They were in the midst of the vision but fearful of the chance to be great. Dare I say we must be mindful not to do the same thing? We must press on to the vision, press on to the greatness that is required of us in this life. Press on to becoming the person God has called us to be. Press on.

The Bible says that the man spoke and said "...Fear not, Daniel, for from the first day that you set your mind *and* heart to understand to humble yourself before your God, your words were heard, and I have come as a consequence of [and in response to] your words. But the prince of the kingdom of Persia withstood me for twenty-one days," reads Daniel 10:12.

Catch the message! The angel said to Daniel that he had been detained for twenty-one days, the exact same number of days Daniel had been praying, fasting, and waiting on the Lord. The angel is letting Daniel know that God hears us.

He also hears you. He knows what you've been waiting for and what you've been going through. God knows that the vision is great and that the burden can be daunting at times. He knows it can be a lonely place, isolating and self-absorbed. He knows it can be exhausting and yet leave one in a state of complete restlessness. God understands the power of a vision. It can seem too big to withstand, too heavy to bear, yet impossible to walk away from.

The Bible says Daniel cried out that he was breathless and without strength due to the vision. Then the Bible says **"Then here touched me again one whose appearance was like that of a man, and he strengthened me."**

The vision that nobody else saw, the vision that Daniel was confessing his weakness to touched him and gave him strength to carry on. This is what the vision does too. It lifts you up. It says that you can make it. It says that you can go on.

The Bible says **"For no temptation (no trial regarded as enticing to sin, no matter how it comes or where it leads) has overtaken you *and* laid hold on you that is beyond human resistance and [that is not adjusted and adapted and belonging to human experience, and such as man can bear]. But God is faithful [to His Word and to His compassionate** nature], and He [can be trusted] not to let you be tempted *and* tried *and* assayed beyond your ability *and* strength of resistance *and* power to endure, but with the temptation He will [always] also provide the way out (the means of escape to a landing place), that you may be capable *and* strong *and* powerful to bear up under it patiently," reads I Corinthians 10:13.

There is a landing place with God. You don't have to be afraid. You don't have to give up your vision because temptation has come along. There is a way of escape. There is a way out. All you have to do is find it, and you will find it when you accept your greatness.

Stop trying to coward away, waiting on a friend to save you. You are the you that you have been waiting for.

So often families find themselves waiting on a savior, somebody to show them the way. So often we search for that light, that someone among us to lift us up, bring us out, or be that beacon of hope, but that someone is you. That beacon of hope is you, the Christ, the God inside you that has given you the vision.

The Bible says "You are the light of the world. A city set on a hill cannot be hidden," reads Matthew 5:14.

The greatness is in you waiting to be utilized, ready to lift you up past the despair, desperation, and need for validation. The greatness is there in you waiting...waiting to be accepted.

REFLECTION QUESTIONS

What vision has God given you for your life? Does it seem too big to handle?

What is stopping you from achieving this vision, if anything?

THE CONCLUSION

---

pursue peace

What then is the end to my story? What does it all come
down to?

I began this story a lifetime ago. I started out
thinking I would write a small book about healing because I
was in a place of pain and needed to be healed. What I found
were two years worth of questions, late nights, and
frustrations.

I hoped that by sharing my piece of truth others
might be able to relate and find their own piece of healing,
truth, and peace along the way.

I wanted this book to mean something, to give
something back, to encourage someone and let others know
that they are not alone in their struggles. But did it work? Was
the journey worth it?

The truth is that I'm still not perfect. I'm still far from
what I hope to be, but I'm here; some days by no fault of my
own. I am a little less scared, a little wiser, a lot more honest,
and a lot less lonely.

You see the truth is that I did find love...twice, and I
lost myself in the process both times. I resented them both in

a way that was bitter and cold, said I forgave them when I knew I didn't.

I was confused, baffled, wondered why they had taken my love and gave so little in return. Our stories were complex, full of dead ends and unanswered questions. The desire for human interaction and relationship had broken me and I was left to put myself back together again

I hid from them, unable to see them for who they are, were, wanted to be, hoped for, and went on to become. I was unable to say "I see you."

And that's when it happened. That's how our story ends. One night I saw him...standing there amidst a crowd of people at a nightclub we use to go to. He looked like his old self again, and for a while we exchanged glances.

JC...

We found ourselves standing next to each other, cordial and smiling; not offended by the other person or fearful the way we use to be.

"Darvin," he said after we had talked for a while. "Would you like to dance with me?"

I barely took time to think.

"Yes," I said, and I never dance.

Still we walked to the dance floor, stood close to one another and listened as the DJ played the last song of the night. The words rippled and vibrated through the night air.

Love you like a brother, treat you like a friend, respect you like a lover...oh-wo, oh-wo-, oh wo...

And so lovers held each other tight and close. And suddenly I found myself falling...into the dip of his shoulder. My eyes were closed, and I am drifting...away. And for the first time in years I am able to breathe in his presence.

I go home elated, and I awake realizing that I had done it. I was able to face my brokenness. In fact I held on tight. And it dawned on me the next morning as I rose that I had freed myself. I had been able to confront my fears, look them in the eyes and had been rewarded with a place of peace, a place of healing. All of this, you see, because I had told the truth. Yes, that's right, I told it, you see...I told the truth.

REFLECTION QUESTIONS

Did you learn to face the truth about yourself?

Are you any close to peace than you were before you started this journey?

What did you learn about yourself?

ABOUT THE AUTHOR

Darvin Lewis is a multi-talented speaker, teacher and author of two captivating books, How Big Is Your Faith and Stop Feeding Crazy & Pursue Peace.

He is a graduate of Specs Howard School of Broadcast Arts as well as Siena Heights University, and is currently completing graduate courses in pastoral studies at Loyola University Chicago. He was awarded Outstanding Talent by the Specs Howard School and went on to receive Honorable Mention by the Michigan Association of Broadcasters for Best College News Feature.

Born in Indianapolis, Indiana, Darvin was drawn to writing at an early age. He taught himself to type and wrote his first screenplay at the age of fourteen.

When he is not writing books Darvin also works as a kindergarten studio instructor and enjoys the opportunity to expand young minds by exploring the world of art.

He enjoys cooking, watching cartoons, and taking walks around the lake behind his home.

NOTES

Notes

Notes

Notes

Notes

Notes

Notes

Notes

Notes

Notes

www.ingramcontent.com/pod-product-compliance
Lightning Source LLC
Chambersburg PA
CBHW061729020426
42331CB00006B/1158

* 9 780989 170901 *